MALLETT'S

GREAT ENGLISH FURNITURE

MALLETT'S

GREAT ENGLISH FURNITURE

Lanto Synge

A BULFINCH PRESS BOOK
LITTLE, BROWN AND COMPANY
BOSTON · TORONTO · LONDON

Things men have made with wakened hand, and put soft life into, are awake through years with transferred touch, and go on glowing for long years.
And for this reason, some old things are lovely,
warm still with the life of forgotten men who made them.
D. H. Lawrence

First North American Edition

ISBN 0-8212-1869-7

Library of Congress Catalog Card Number 91-55477
Library of Congress Cataloging-in-Publication information is available.

Bulfinch Press is an imprint and trademark of
Little, Brown and Company (Inc.)

Published simultaneously in Canada by
Little, Brown & Company (Canada) Limited

PRINTED IN SPAIN

1 (Frontispiece) A view in one of the Mallett's showrooms shows a Queen Anne bureau bookcase bearing a maker's label attributing it to John Belchier. Two walnut armchairs of the same period are also shown, one upholstered with fine needlework. The Regency writing table is decorated with moulded brass panels and has lyre-shaped end supports.

CONTENTS

PREFACE

*T*his volume celebrates some of the achievements of Mallett, the antiques business of New Bond Street and Bourdon House in London, at the time of its 125th anniversary. The book presents an anthology of photographs drawn from a large archive built up over more than 50 years. Most of the colour illustrations are from the last two decades. Before this we were chiefly dependent on black and white images and the company has an extensive black and white photographic library. In more recent times we have handled many great treasures and happily we have colour representations of these. The Mallett catalogues of the 1920s and 1930s also provide an interesting record of past treasures which, when compared with today's stock, show changing tastes.

In this book I attempt to outline the history of English furniture using for reference some of the finest examples that Mallett has been lucky enough to handle. I also illustrate a selection of splendid rarities, which stand out in terms of quality, but also reflect generally the times in which they were created. Some cross-references are made to continental furniture, showing how ideas from various countries influenced England at different times. A few spectacular items of Dutch, French and Italian craftsmanship are included to reflect this relationship. A book of this kind cannot be wholly comprehensive, but I hope it gives a general picture of the development of fine English furniture over more than three hundred years, and shows the gentle shifts of preference in different generations.

In preparing the book I have had valuable help from my fellow directors, other members of the company, and from our clients. I am grateful to all the owners of the pieces shown, especially since many photographs have been reproduced without consulting them – a process which would have been impracticable. The photographs, however, are our own. Many of the more recent ones were taken by our resident photographer Clive Bartlett, and special thanks are due to him for his beautiful work. Thanks are also due to his predecessors.

I am most grateful also to Gina Synge and Sarah West, and to my publishers for inviting me to compile this book.

2 The front showroom at Mallett's in New Bond Street displays a variety of English furniture. The wrought-iron gates were adapted from a design found in a French cathedral.

allett is probably the largest antique shop that deals in important English furniture together with fine decorative items and unusual objects of excellence. Many passers-by in Bond Street are familiar with the facade and may pause to admire furniture displayed in the large curved windows, but few suspect the extent of the shop within – 11 quite substantial rooms. A second business is sited nearby at Bourdon House. We also incorporate the Christopher Wood Gallery, and have a department specialising in fine glass.

Mallett and Son (Antiques) Ltd has changed considerably in size, scope, and intent since its foundation in 1865 by John Mallett (a jeweller and silversmith), at 36 Milsom Street, Bath, Somerset. His son, Walter Mallett, who had joined his father's business in the 1870s or early 1850s, quickly assumed complete control, and today he is acknowledged as the real founder of the firm. It was he who expanded the stock to include old silver and furniture and who arranged for the purchase of the lease of the Octagon in Bath.

This remarkable building had originally been designed as a church in 1767 by the architect Thomas Lightholder, whose specific brief was to produce a structure which would be warm, comfortable, and well lit. The Octagon fulfilled all those requirements, and it became the most fashionable church in

3 Another room at Mallett's is furnished with a spectacular Chippendale giltwood landscape mirror, English lacquer cabinets and a pair of Chinese mirror pictures.

Bath. Eminent and distinguished visitors made a point of engaging a pew for as long as they stayed in the city, hiring it at the same time as they hired their lodgings. The most expensive of these pews were like small rooms, each with its own fireplace and easy chairs. Between service and sermon, an interval was allowed during which footmen tended to the fires and saw that their master and mistress were comfortable. The vaults of this building were let out to a wine merchant, which gave rise to lines by Anstey:

> Spirits above and spirits below,
> Spirits of Bliss and spirits of Woe,
> The Spirits above are Spirits Divine,
> The Spirits below are Spirits of Wine.

Since the building was leasehold, it was never consecrated, so when it fell into disuse in the 1890s an opportunity arose for Mallett's to take it over with the minimum of difficulty. New showrooms were built on each side of the church, with workshops and storage in the basement. A gas engine was installed to drive the polishing lathes, work the lift, make the electric light, and, by means of a fan, circulate air through every part of the building. As communications improved, express trains from London to the West Country facilitated journeys to the spa, and brought much added interest and business to Mallett's at the Octagon. It soon became the foremost antique business in the West Country, and widely known.

In 1908 the Franco-British Exhibition was held at Earls Court in London, and Mallett's took a stand there. This was such a successful venture that Walter Mallett decided to open a permanent shop in London, and he took a lease on premises at 40 New Bond Street.

On Walter Mallett's death in 1930, the business passed to a consortium of six of his employees, who in 1937 decided to close the Octagon premises and move the whole business to London. Francis Mallett became chairman. He advanced the business considerably in every respect, and was noted as one of the foremost connoisseurs of his day. He was a keen collector of clocks, watches, and Oriental ivories, and on his death he left a large part of his collection to the Ashmolean Museum at Oxford.

In 1955 Francis Egerton took over the chairmanship, and it was from this date that Mallett's began to assume its present form. There was no longer any direct family involvement in the company, and, having brought in two new directors, Francis Egerton was free to develop the business to conform to his own exacting requirements. The hallmarks of his approach were an insistence on the highest quality in every sphere, a meticulous attention to detail, and the deliberate projection of a highly personal, decorative taste.

4 This scarlet lacquer bureau bookcase, standing on legs, was made in England in the early part of the 18th century. The side chairs have the same origin and are part of a large set attributed to Giles Grendy and perhaps made for export to a Spanish duke.

Various rearrangements of rooms on several floors at 40 New Bond Street became consolidated in what are now the famous showrooms on two floors at ground and basement level. Three rooms represent the last remaining shop interiors by the architect Raymond Erith, and have recently been listed by the Department of the Environment with support from English Heritage to save them for posterity.

From here pieces have travelled to museums and private collections all over the world. Mallett's is particularly proud of its close association with the major international museums. The Victoria and Albert Museum possesses more than 50 pieces of furniture which at one time or another formed part of the stock at 40 New Bond Street, and many items have gone to American museums. I shall say more about our contribution to public and private collections in my final chapter.

Complementary to the important furniture are Mallett's special productions – lamps and exclusive low tables of a timeless design incorporating and framing special decorative or antique features. These are part of our approach to furnishing with an eye for quality, and an insistence on an overall decorative effect.

The site around 40 New Bond Street is about to be redeveloped, so Mallett's showrooms will be put in wraps for a few years while work continues. In the meantime the business will move to a fine building offering new opportunities at 141 New Bond Street. The company expects to return to the showrooms at No 40 in due course.

Mallett's second business was established in 1962 at Bourdon House, in the heart of Mayfair. Until 1953 this was the London house of the 2nd Duke of Westminster and it has an interesting history. Built for William Burdon in the years 1723-25, during the reign of George I, the house stood amidst fields and market-gardens between the emerging Berkeley and Hanover Squares.

The property came into the family of the future Dukes of Westminster in 1677, through the marriage of Sir Thomas Grosvenor to Miss Mary Davies (hence Davies Street), the beautiful daughter of a local yeoman. Nearly 50 years later this land was leased to the Burdons who, shortly afterwards, started to build a house there. Bourdon House still retains the character of a 250-year-old family home. Within its period setting there are three floors and many good panelled rooms filled with French and other continental furniture, objets d'art, bibelots, and decorative pictures. The stock is more eclectic than that at Bond Street; it includes rare masterpieces together with unusual and exotic items and other pieces of eccentric interest. On the third floor there is an octagonal treasure room where fascinating Indian gold tribal jewellery is displayed. Although this volume must be limited chiefly to English furniture, some other European examples must be included to represent the considerable number of important French, German, Dutch and Swedish pieces that have passed through our hands. These also demonstrate the interplay of influences on and by English furniture in the various times of political and social strength.

The paved garden provides a perfect backdrop for antique garden statuary, ornaments, and furniture – another special feature of the business.

In 1983 the present team of five directors – David Nickerson, Peter Maitland, Lanto Synge, Peter Dixon and John Yorke – took over management of the company; and in order to secure necessary financial strength Mallett's subsequently became a publicly-owned company.

In 1988 the business acquired the Christopher Wood Gallery. Christopher Wood opened his gallery in Motcomb Street in 1979. It specializes in fine Victorian, Edwardian, and Pre-Raphaelite paintings, watercolours, and drawings.

Within Bourdon House and New Bond Street there is ample room to display a great variety of antiques. The stock comprises furniture, including mirrors, pictures, and objects. Occasionally, when the opportunity arises to acquire something remarkable outside our field we have very special items beyond the bounds of even our eclectic range. One such occurrence was a fascinating collection of five mid-15th-century dorsaria of the East Anglian School. These were frescos which had been transferred to panels having been saved from a disused church in Norfolk. The various sections showed biblical subjects with delightful simplicity and elegance in pleasing earthen tones, predominantly yellow and red ochre. Illustrated in fig 5 is one of the scenes, the Flight into Egypt; the dimensions are 6ft 2½in x 5ft 5½in.

Each of the rooms in the Mallett shops is carefully arranged to recreate the atmosphere of a private house; furniture is exhibited with an eye to the general effect, and care is taken to place every piece in such a way as to complement its neighbour and show it in an exemplary room setting. Within the general layouts, rooms are arranged as dining rooms, with tables and sets of chairs, as well as sideboards or console tables against the walls. There is a panelled library with bookcases, desks, and library tables. Two more rooms, with period pine panelling, contain a fine collection of walnut and early 18th-century furniture, while other areas are designed as drawing rooms or reception rooms of a more general nature. A grotto at Bond Street, conceived on Italianate lines by Raymond Erith, walls encrusted with shells, currently displays items from the new glass department. A smaller exotic room at Bourdon House has glass cabinets filled with small treasures. From time to time in the garden magnificent stone dragons of colossal weight seem to fly in

5 One of a very fine set of five mid-15th-century dorsaria from East
Anglia, saved from a disused Norfolk Church. This fresco depicts the
Flight into Egypt.

and out. Sometimes it's a bird cage, large enough to live in, or some other large and splendid object which is hoisted into position over the old 18th-century walls. Smaller sculptures, urns, and busts may be viewed through the garden gate, and at night if one is passing, they seem to be murmuring convivially in the moonlight, pleased that the daytime's busy streets are quiet.

It is part of Mallett's philosophy that as well as each item being a fine antique it should be part of a creative whole, and that the making of interiors is in itself a true art form.

A large part of the fun of being an antique dealer is in helping clients in the artistic pursuit of creating a fine home, where each area and wall space becomes a well thought-out contribution to an overall atmosphere of beauty and interest combined with practicality. Some rooms may be grand and showy, displaying magnificent objects unashamedly in a museum-like presentation, while others will be more domestic, though thoughtfully arranged, and filled with carefully selected items, each one 'saying' something individual. Each will have, in addition to usefulness, an element of pleasing charm and relevance that will contribute to the room, house and life in general. Fine pieces of furniture are works of art and works of art communicate. That is what I mean by emphasising that each piece ought to say something. In the same metaphoric language my partners and I, in selecting stock for the shop, are sometimes heard to comment when rejecting a piece, 'I'm sorry, it doesn't speak to me'.

Part of this communication is of course a matter of taste, and Mallett's have developed a hallmark of style and taste which is very idiosyncratic. It is based on the highest possible ratings of excellence in style and quality. Our job is to provide 'the best available'. For me, as one of the Mallett team, the greatest fascination (other than the obvious fun of dealing with people) has been seeing, even over a period of only 20 years or so, distinct movements in taste, definite changes in what is considered the most desirable, the most beautiful, and usually therefore the most valuable. Here lies the living part of antique dealing and collecting. Although the best will always hold its own, fashions create interesting waverings of fortune. Queen Anne walnut furniture has always been highly regarded, but elaborately carved, dark brown mahogany furniture of the mid-18th century, for example, was slightly neglected in the 1970s while painted furniture was especially valued. Fine lacquered furniture is now perhaps relatively ignored in favour of magnificent Sheraton satinwood. This is undoubtedly a time of fine woods and inlay.

The antiques themselves are of course the focus of Mallett's livelihood; artefacts created by past generations to standards that often seem incredible to us today might easily be taken for granted as a business commodity. But even in the hubbub of a hectic commercial organisation we never forget that most pieces of furniture or objets d'art are, by the very fact of their survival, a remarkable testament to human creativity. Amongst these the finest examples, which have been sifted and selected from the wider treasure house, are humbling in all respects. They are wonderfully conceived and crafted with a vision, design, style, quality, and workmanship that is usually far beyond any of our own abilities. On any level we should value these pieces tremendously and remind ourselves just how lucky we are to live in this age and be the beneficiaries of such a legacy, which is a great part of the joy of being. Some of us could scarcely imagine an existence without 'things'.

Our clients come from all over the world. With England being so rich in works of art accumulated over centuries from all over the world, it is right and appropriate that London remains the centre of the art market. Frequently we see important pieces of different origins brought to London for sale, including fine English furniture which was exported to France, Italy, or Spain in the 18th or 19th century or to the United States of America in more recent times. Many great pieces of furniture have come to Mallett's from the USA, from old clients, to be offered again to prospective new owners, so our mutual heritage is frequently recirculated. A sub-plot of this book shows how foreign furniture and objects have always played a part in English houses. Furniture and treasures have been imported from European and Oriental countries from at least as far back as the 17th century, and these things have formed an important and influential part of our heritage.

About one third of our clients are English, another third American, and the remainder come from continental Europe and other parts of the world. Australians have recently taken a greater interest in fine furniture. It is a common misapprehension that good pieces often go to the difficult climates of Arab countries, but this is not true. In all my time with the business I never once remember having furniture sent to the Middle East. We do, however, have some clients with Arab connections, but usually they also live in London, Paris, or New York.

As antique dealers, we are fully aware of our duties in offering opportunities of acquiring wonderful furniture to all who come to us. Our commercial instincts are linked with passing on the trusteeship of historic and irreplaceable objects to new owners who will treasure and look after them for a period ranging from a few years to a lifespan or even many generations. Like those in other professional fields, we have an acquired experience as well as personal aptitude and we use this to offer what we consider to be the finest antiques available in a sympathetic and creatively stimulating setting.

Fine furniture must always be properly maintained, and inevitably will need some attention and restoration from time to time. Occasionally pieces may have fallen out of fashion in the past and been stored away in attics or stables, or otherwise neglected. We therefore have workshops at Bourdon House where a dozen full-time craftsmen carry out necessary work. Under careful supervision, inspected several times each day, tired pieces can be gently coaxed back into the full vigours of life, while other items need only minor attention to loose veneers or a healthy wax polishing. Paintwork and lacquer restoration calls for especially patient and judicious work as the charm and mystery of the old patination on such surfaces can be ruined very quickly by wrong or insensitive treatment. As well as our loyal and long-serving team of restorers at Bourdon House, we call upon a wide network of outside workshops all over London. At these workshops highly-skilled craftsmen undertake a very broad range of activities ranging from metalwork and glass to leather and textiles, in addition to carrying out surplus cabinet repairs and polishing (fig 6).

In this anthology of some of the finest furniture and objects handled by Mallett's over many years I shall attempt to describe them in approximately historical sequence. It is hard to select relatively few examples from the hundreds of fine pieces which have passed through our doors. But I hope to provide a reasonably comprehensive historical collection, together with a survey of fine English furniture chosen from amongst the very best of Mallett's 125-year history.

6 An unattributed oil painting shows a polisher of antique furniture working amongst the delightful clutter of his trade.

THE LATE SEVENTEENTH CENTURY

*O*ur period, for practical purposes, begins more or less around the time of the joint accession to the English throne of William of Orange and his cousin Mary, in 1688. William and Mary's names, as a joint term, have become a significant label for the beginning of a new domestic feeling in English furniture, with a stylistic cohesion that perhaps reflects the idea of home rather than castle. It was not a sudden change, as the Caroline age had already reflected a more domestic air, but the last decade or so of the 17th century was a time when greater efforts were made towards the general furnishing of rooms. Comfort was desired, partly for practicality, and partly for show, as a display of extravagant opulence. These years saw the beginnings of what we now call interior decoration.

The other distinctive feature of late 17th-century furniture in England was the adoption of French and Dutch innovations, heralding new fashions of design, a new wave of craftsmanship and techniques, and a greater understanding of the riches of materials which could be imported from Europe. A relatively sudden revolution in the decorative arts, as in architecture, art, music, and costume, undoubtedly began with the new confidence following the restoration of Charles II. But most significant was the stimulation caused by the arrival of Huguenot, Dutch, and French immigrants who brought invigorating ideas and influences, together with

7 A splendid Chinese lacquer cabinet imported to England towards the end of the 17th century has here been mounted on a carved giltwood stand and been given a rich cresting. This is representative of the rich combination of English and Oriental furniture used in English houses at the time of William and Mary's reign.

useful expertise in design and craftsmanship. These indeed were to shape the future of our decorative arts in an unprecedented and uniquely successful manner. The good fortune of this influential invasion was that the mood and tempo admirably suited the evolving English taste. The new fashions, a composite of Dutch and French, were appropriate both at Court and in a more domestic setting. The ornateness of some Charles II baroque interiors and furniture, for example, had a hallmark of confident, ostentatious, gilt grandeur. But during the reign of William and Mary the grandeur became more controlled, simpler, less exuberant, but still remained noble.

Hampton Court Palace, which was largely remodelled for William and Mary by Christopher Wren, has an obvious, massive grandeur in its architectural scale; but the fine stonework pilasters, pediments, and windows of the facades, together with the military avenues of trees and orderly flower beds around the building, reflect noble pomp attuned to the gentle and comfortably restrained grandeur of Purcell's music. Inside the palace the superbly proportioned state rooms and small intimate lobbies alike are each discreetly but luxuriously lined with oak panelling of the highest quality. This was an excellent background for the tapestries, carpets, mirrors, and furniture which were placed against the walls as a setting for the finely dressed courtiers who paraded through them.

The great virtue of the new Dutch and Huguenot influence was that it also appealed to the nobility and gentry whose style of living was that of the courtiers rather than the Court. They did not require pretentious surroundings, but wanted to build and furnish houses in a manner which would impress their peers and which would give them pride and enable them to display and enjoy a degree of luxury.

It was in this context that English furniture of the latter part of the 17th-century developed its highly personable character. How did it differ from earlier domestic furniture? Furniture of the earlier part of the century was usually made of solid oak, dark and weighty to our eyes today. It was sometimes finally carved and occasionally inlaid with pieces of lighter coloured woods such as holly; but because it was hard to work, it was more often crude in form with rough carving and joining. Very often oak furniture was partly built into the fabric of the room for which it was conceived. Some pieces seen today have been adapted from such situations. Many others are often much altered or adapted by 'antiquarians' of the 18th and 19th centuries, as well as by dealers of more recent times trying to save residual remnants.

The use of walnut as a solid wood, and subsequently as a veneer, developed from about 1650. At first it was used concurrently with oak for making tables, chairs, and stools, and it was often difficult to tell the difference. But it was more suitable for intricate carving and it had a richer colour that responded well to polishing which quickly gave it a superiority. Walnut soon became a goldmine and the basis of the glory of William and Mary and subsequent 18th-century furniture.

Cabinets, chests, knee-hole desks, bureaux, bureau bookcases, bookcases, and mirror frames, as well as chairs of many kinds and a host of other less usual and smaller pieces, were made of walnut. Sometimes the timber was extravagantly used in its solid form; indeed it had to be used in this way to give strength to chair or cabinet legs, certain mouldings and other elements. Often, however, especially well-figured wood was sawn into thin sheets to be used as a covering veneer over plainer construction woods such as oak or pine. Walnut, and other prized but less extensively used woods such as yew, mulberry, and elm, were chosen for making into veneer on account of their burr markings. These dense curly patterns are caused in wood grain where there is an irregular growth on the side of a tree or bough. In addition to plain veneering the William and Mary period saw a very wide variety in furniture decoration; indeed it is true to say that few original forms have developed since the late 17th century. Marquetry and parquetry were developed out of experiments in the use of contrasting woods. Richest of all was furniture covered with embossed silver; this had been known in certain special royal circumstances earlier in the century. But now all of the following were sometimes to be seen on furniture: Chinese lacquer, Japanese lacquer, European lacquer (known as japanning), ivory, tortoishell, shagreen (animal or fish skins), painting, needlework, rolled paperwork, gilding, and silvering. In other special circumstances, woodwork might provide the supporting framework for the display of oil painted canvas, panels of pietra dura (pictures made of semi-precious stones) or verre eglomisé (coloured and gilded mirror glass). All these would usually be combined with contrasting carved elements, frames, mouldings, legs and crestings.

However, the decoration most closely associated with Holland was the use of marquetry. Marquetry involved inlaying small pieces of contrasting – sometimes dyed – veneers, in pictorial format. Pieces of ivory and other materials were frequently incorporated. Parquetry was the use of veneers or solid pieces laid, in geometrical formation usually in a largish scale. Stone and marble had long been used in this way in buildings and floors, of course, were made in similar fashion. The format was now used in a smaller scale on flat furniture surfaces.

Fig 8 shows a table of about 1690 with many admirable features of the period. The legs are solid walnut turned in barley sugar form and terminating

in ball feet, a noted feature of the period. The rest of the table has an oak frame finely veneered in walnut. The drawer front and sides have straight veneers, but the stretcher and top are elaborately decorated with oyster veneers and marquetry. Oyster veneers, showing tree rings like an oyster shell, are made by slicing the wood from small boughs across the grain. The roundels are then laid in regular (usually circular) patterns, within bandings of cross-grain veneers. As was often the case at this time these richly mellow veneers are combined with panels of marquetry, usually of repeating floral design. Various lighter and darker woods were used together with brightly dyed pieces to represent flowers, and with pieces of other materials – especially ivory, ebony, and tortoishell – to give stronger contrasts. As in this case, the green has survived better than the red and blue which were also prominent at one time.

Occasionally one can see the original effect on an interior fitment within a cabinet or drawer which has not been exposed to light. But to our eyes today it is the naturally faded and patinated surfaces, as on this table top, which seem right. We might not like the original if it were spirited back to us, any more than we would the richly decorated medieval sculpture and monuments that once made our gothic cathedrals look bright or even gaudy.

The pair of side chairs in fig 9 have a 17th-century formality and stiffness,

8 A William and Mary table with oyster veneers elaborately decorated with marquetry.

but they are elegant with a definite upright emphasis, perhaps allowing for close proximity around a table or against a wall. They are of solid walnut – although they could equally have been of oak – and are finely carved with delicate scrolls and pierced crestings. The backs and seats are woven with split cane. The fine mesh was replaced early on by a broader weave. These chairs, in their stiff, elegant, Dutch formality, show the influence of Daniel Marot, a Huguenot, whose designs played a significant part in the history of English furniture.

A magnificent pair of japanned William and Mary armchairs is shown in fig 10. These generous beechwood chairs have fine-mesh carving in the backs and seats, and the carved frames show the best sculptural elements of the period. Bold scrolls form the legs and armrests while the panels of the backs are flanked by turned columns. The crestings at the tops of the chairs and the stretchers joining the front legs are in the form of elaborate pieced arches made up of scrolling mouldings incorporating coronets. The crestings also show what seems to be a double-headed eagle. The painted decoration, a kind of chinoiserie, consists of a black background richly powdered with gilt, described with polychrome lines and floral detailing.

Even grander, but also showing elements of Daniel Marot's influence, with a feeling for rich upholstery, is the pair of chairs in fig 11. These are of

9 and 10 Two pairs of late 17th-century chairs each with characteristically high backs. The pair on the left are carved in walnut, while the armchairs are of beechwood japanned in imitation of oriental lacquer.

beechwood, suitable for the preparation of the gilding. They retain the original gesso which is laid over carved mouldings and then itself carved with detailing. This was then overlaid with water gilding and burnished. The chairs are also remarkable in that they retain their original red velvet coverings with elaborate fringes. Stretchers on chairs and tables are a feature of William and Mary furniture, but are less common on furniture of the early 18th century. The very elegant rake, or deep backward curve, of the back legs of these chairs should be noted.

'Mystery' is an immeasurable characteristic of many 17th-century houses, interiors, textiles, and furniture. Fig 12 shows a cabinet on stand entirely veneered not with wood, or painted decoration, but with shagreen, a kind of leather – in this case the polished skin of ray fish. The material was probably dyed a bright blue-green but has now faded to this stone-like effect. The piece is an example of the love for natural substances, often introduced with exotic originality, and sometimes combined with contrasting settings of silver or other rich materials. Tortoishell and ivory were the most frequent natural substances used in lavish decoration.

Leather was not only used for cushions and similar household purposes. It was also used for decoration, as in the case of magnificent book bindings, because it could easily take dyes of many colours or gold tooling. Sometimes larger objects were made with leather coverings. In furniture it is rare except on trunks. Fig 13 shows a splendid trunk of about 1670 attributed to Richard Pigge, coffer maker to Charles II. The domed top and front are elaborately

11 (opposite) A magnificent pair of giltwood side chairs, circa 1690, retaining their original red velvet upholstery and fringing.

12 (above) A late 17th-century cabinet entirely overlaid with shagreen faded to a mysterious grey-green.

decorated with brass nailing while the brass hinges, lock escutcheon, and other mounts are shaped with crowns and richly engraved. Some 80 years later this treasured piece was given a fine carved mahogany stand in order to confirm its place as a piece of furniture worthy of permanence.

One of the most fascinating aspects of the history of furniture is the interplay between East and West. Europeans have always had a fascination for the Orient and the to and fro of influences in decoration is endless. Spices, lacquer, textiles and porcelain were all imported into Europe from the 17th century onwards. These items were very much prized in households as prestigious and decorative. If genuine imported pieces could not be obtained, or as a supplement to them, imitations would be supplied by merchants or even made by members of a household in order to delight in the fashion for exotic fantasies of the East. Everything was termed by the general word 'Indian' and no distinction was made between Chinese, Japanese, or true Indian. The use of the imported pieces was often unrelated to their original purpose, and little effort was made to be too correct about the manner in which panels of lacquer, textiles, or porcelain were used in the copies. Lacquer, especially, was nearly always combined with other materials in the construction of furniture or for wall panels. Lacquer screens became very popular – both genuine Chinese ones and European copies.

I shall devote a later chapter to lacquer, but here fig 7 (page 18) shows a splendid Chinese lacquer cabinet of a kind that was regularly imported in the late 17th century. Many copies of exactly the same proportions were made,

13 A Charles II leather trunk decorated with brass mounts and nailing and supplied in the 18th century with a carved mahogany stand.

with a similar layout of drawers inside; only close inspection tells us the true origin. In this case, the cabinet being Chinese, the woodwork can be seen to be of poor quality and of very light and insubstantial timber, not the oak of which English copies were made. The joints on the drawers do not have the neat dovetails of English furniture but a cruder form of splicing. The metal mounts combine good quality engraved brasswork, perhaps an English replacement, and also the lighter weight, almost tinny corner pieces characteristic of Chinese examples. The lacquer decoration, however, has the real authenticity, quality, and charm of Chinese lacquer at its best, with a fine, balanced, but un-English combination of ideas worked in a variety of tones on the front. The cabinet, as was the fashion in Europe, is seen mounted on a very fine English giltwood base and given an elaborate giltwood cresting. Such a grand presentation as this shows how highly valued lacquer cabinets were.

Many cabinets of this kind have survived – both Chinese and European. There are also a number of Japanese examples. However, it is rare to find a complete piece of furniture still intact with its base and with the gilt cresting. In many cases the gilt cresting, if there was one, has been lost. This is an especially fine example and it has passed through Mallett's twice. The cresting is somewhat architectural in appearance, having a mask in the centre and elaborate floral scrollwork flanked by a pair of obelisks. The base is also immensely grand and appears to have the initials 'AA' incorporated in the strapwork decoration. It is interesting to notice how the stretchers carry five small platforms on which small oriental vases – probably blue and white – would have been placed. Standing behind the cabinet can be seen part of a large screen which interestingly also combines East and West. The central panels are of Chinese hand painted wallpaper decorated with flowers and birds, and clearly made for export to Europe. These have been mounted together with panels of real oriental lacquer at top and bottom and within a European framework of imitation lacquer known as 'japanning'. A treatise on japanning was published by Stalker and Parker in 1688. This, essentially, was a small manual for the guidance of professionals and amateurs alike who wished to imitate the oriental lacquer which they saw being imported into Europe.

Fig 14 shows another fascinating mixture of English and oriental ideas. This is a mirror in a large painted frame of characteristic Dutch and English format but entirely decorated with very curious and idiosyncratic motifs. The cresting has a wide arc of pierced fretwork. Below this is a large window containing a coat of arms made of rolled paper. This filigree work is regularly to be seen on smaller items but rarely in a piece as large as this. Other little

windows in the frame of the mirror show fascinating representations of houses and flowers, also worked in rolled paper and here with shell decoration. The rest of the woodwork is entirely japanned in oriental fashion, imitating the mystery and charm that is characteristic of so many pieces of the late 17th century.

A much richer and more expensive technique was developed in France and became popular in royal and noble houses in England. This is *verre eglomisé,* developed by a Monsieur Glom. The technique consists of decorating glasswork from behind with gilding and coloured foils, providing the frames of mirrors, for example, with a rich, colourful, and glittering appearance. A few of these very grand pieces have survived and some wonderful examples are to be seen at Hampton Court Palace, at Chatsworth, at Penshurst Place, and in other private collections. Mallett's have handled very fine examples including a superb pair of pier glasses with red eglomisé borders, and with their original shaped crestings in the same technique (fig 16). All the panels of red eglomisé are richly decorated with gilded motifs reminiscent of Daniel Marot, including strapwork, lambrequins, tassles, flowers, and swags.

A fascinating aspect of the history of the decorative arts in England is the contrast of the very grand (as represented by such eglomisé mirrors) with the more domestic, though still beautifully made, minor masterpieces. An example of the latter is an outstanding Charles II stumpwork mirror (fig 15). The highly valued mirror plate is set within a shaped frame, entirely covered with raised stumpwork embroidery. Dating from about 1670, this is a particularly fine example of a popular kind of work which was almost always done by young girls who had already completed needlework samplers and perhaps a needlework casket as well. Generally the motifs depicted were very repetitive and were obviously chosen from pattern books or drawn out by art

14 and 15 Two precious mirror glasses framed in the late 17th century with amateur decoration. Fig 14 shows a japanned surround while fig 15 has a frame of embroidered stump work.

masters, but in each case they are worked differently and charmingly reflect the individual characteristics of the little girl's own taste. As in this example, motifs worked included vignettes such as a lady playing a musical instrument within a tent, a king and a queen greeting each other, lions, unicorns, birds, flowers, fishes, castles, and temples.

This particular mirror is in a splendid state of preservation, and between the needlework 'spot' motifs the background is dotted with small sequins,

16 A magnificent pair of tall pier mirrors framed in scarlet and gold verre eglomisé borders, with crestings. Circa 1690.

pieces of mica, and seed pearls which have miraculously survived and not fallen off. The colours of this needlework mirror have become considerably muted, although they are still recognisable. Beadwork of the same period does not fade at all, and to our eyes often seems a little harsh or garish, although magnificent in its own way. This mirror was similarly very bright originally, being embroidered with coloured silks, and framing a fresh piece of mercury mirror-plate which has now become clouded, grey, and somewhat mysterious. We have to set it in the context of all the new textiles and sumptuous works of art which were put in rooms lined with dark oak panelling, creating an atmosphere glittering with richness. As well as the items already referred to, we must picture the brilliant costumes, quantities of silver, the bright porcelain, jewels, highly polished brass, and oriental carpets.

Glass was another facet of wealthy 17th-century life. Recently at Mallett's we have had a splendid collection of extremely rare early English crystal glass, some of it made between 1675 and 1680 by John Ravenscroft. These beautiful rarities which have miraculously survived three centuries include a magnificent pair of tall 'crizzled' vases with contemporary silver-gilt mounts, and a number of smaller items all displaying early attempts at making fine glass and reflecting pleasing shapes reminiscent of contemporary silver utensils (fig 17).

Before leaving the 17th century, I must mention one other item which, although not English, is one of the greatest pieces of furniture we have been fortunate enough to handle (fig 18). A highly important mid-17th-century Florentine piece, the ebonised oak cabinet is decorated with exceptional pietra dura panels depicting on the upper section birds perched on flowering trees, flanked by two landscape scenes, with rare panels of fruit below. The

17 A group of 'crizzled' glass pieces, being the spectacular achievement of John Ravenscroft around 1680 in his attempt to make clear glass.

18 A magnificent pietra dura cabinet entirely inset with fine Florentine specimen marble pictures.

front of the cabinet also has columns veneered with lapis lazuli, and gilt bronze capitals. The sides of the cabinet are inlaid with panels of Tuscan albarese and inset geometrically with semi-precious stones. There are numerous drawers and an interior studded with enamels and inscribed plaques. The imagery depicted on this magnificent cabinet is reminiscent of pattern books and herbals of the 16th and 17th centuries, and many of the motifs are also seen in woodwork, needlework, and decorative painting. This sumptuous piece of furniture was probably made by a German craftsman working for the Medicis, or for a patron who had collected the pietra dura panels. It is possible that he had the top section made first and then ordered the lower section to support the main body of the cabinet.

THE AGE
OF WALNUT

*T*he 18th century witnessed the epitome of elegance. It brings to mind the simple flowing lines of a Queen Anne chair, Robert Adam's refined, classical buildings, silk, satin, and Sheraton interiors. We can imagine the beautifully dressed women and elegant men wearing fine embroidery, conveyed in carriages or sedan chairs in the great Georgian cities of Bath, Edinburgh or Dublin. Baroque flamboyance seemed an ostentation of the past. This was a time of lightness, of the music of Handel, Arne, and Mozart. Merriness and frivolity appeared to pervade everything, and yet this was not the case at all. The 18th century was, of course, just as full of brutality, poverty, long drawn-out and bitter wars, corruption, and social unfairness. Nevertheless, in England as in much of Europe, there was certainly a long period of creativity in the decorative arts. Interior decoration was now fully established. Architects, who also filled the role of interior designers, created whole rooms. Throughout the 18th century, they were the most important instigators of design; and, as such, had a great influence on furniture – both direct and indirect. It was also a period of great social development. Rich patrons took on exciting new projects. The finest furniture was made during this 100-year span, and the many surviving pieces of this period form the most significant body of what we regard as antique furniture today.

I have said that the overriding spirit of 18th-century antique furniture – as

19 A group of early 18th-century walnut and lacquer furniture with a crewelwork curtain.

of the other decorative arts of the period – is one of elegance. Yet, we must appreciate how certain extreme innovations would have come as a considerable shock. Some of the new ideas, wild creations of decoration and furniture making, must have seemed extraordinarily ostentatious and bizarre. Rococo furniture, with its playful scrolls, flowers and cascades, reflected something of the rocky cascading of Roman grottoes. It was a fanciful form full of glorious showmanship, which was sometimes carried to absurd limits. These included the whimsies of chinoiserie, where anything oriental was imitated semi-mockingly in idyllic fantasies.

Another extreme was the Gothic Revival. Deriving from serious medieval ecclesiastical architecture, the Gothic style was taken up in light-hearted, superficial, almost humorous, decorative features. These were disciplined within Georgian proportions, and the true architectural purposes of supporting arches and such elements were dismissed in favour of airy, decorative pattern-making. Rococo chinoiserie and gothic fantasies, especially on a large scale or in entire rooms, must have been shockingly ostentatious. They were however contained within the calm proportions of Georgian good manners. We have now learned to look upon them as an expected part of 18th-century decorative progression. I am sure that when the large, showy cabinet in fig 133 was made, it must have caused gasps at its opulence, and perhaps horror at its strange oriental temple appearance. Its complicated fenestration and gilded icicles were avant garde and the piece was made on an unusually large scale, enough in itself to cause wonder. We shall return to this piece (see page 118) having considered the origins of this extraordinary pinnacle of English furniture.

I must now go back to the earlier part of the 18th century when the use of native English walnut was so prized. The reign of Queen Anne (1701-1714) is renowned for simple, elegant lines and an emphasis on fine woods, especially walnut and oak – with gilding, upholstery, lacquering, painting and other recognised finishes. The Queen Anne period, which in furniture terms comprises roughly the first two decades of the 18th century, is one of domesticity, of smallish rooms containing relatively neat cabinet pieces. These were not elaborately decorated, but were finely proportioned and had a certain elegant simplicity of line which contributed to making the whole ensemble especially commendable. There is nothing more appealing to us than the characteristically small-sized, yet well-proportioned, walnut chest of drawers, knee-hole desk, or bureau, each of which would fit into any room in any period. As a result, walnut furniture has never fallen seriously out of fashion but has been treasured by generation after generation. In some cases it may have been rejected by the gentry who wished to inhabit more opulent,

grander surroundings; but these compact pieces of furniture were often rescued and survived in smaller houses or in the attics of great houses. Although much furniture was badly treated or heavily altered or repaired, a great deal has survived.

Unfortunately walnut is especially prone to woodworm, and in almost every case the feet have been eaten away and have had to be replaced. It is rare to find a piece of early 18th-century walnut furniture which does not have some signs of the dreaded beetle; indeed if I were ever to see a piece without some old woodworm, I might even doubt its authenticity. One of the greatest advantages of mahogany when it began to be imported a few decades later was that it was not attractive to woodworm; indeed it is very rarely attacked as the wood is too hard.

In the same way that Queen Anne houses have a comfortable squareness, so also do many of the small pieces of cabinet furniture so typical of the first two decades of the 18th century. I have selected here a few items which are special and representative of the many fine pieces that Mallett's has been fortunate enough to have in stock.

Fig 20 shows a small chest of drawers with four long drawers and a brushing slide above. The walnut burr veneers chosen for the drawer fronts and top have, over the years, developed a superb patination and wonderfully

20 This Queen Anne period walnut-veneered chest of drawers has faded to an especially delightful colour.

21, 22 and 23 Three representative early 18th-century walnut chests, all with neat compact proportions. Fig 21 (left) shows Dutch influence; fig 22 (right) is a bachelor's chest with a folding top; and fig 23 (below) is a knee-hole desk.

mellow uneven colour which is the unique quality of walnut. The sides of the chest are of straight walnut veneers and the whole piece is of oak and pine construction. The drawers are entirely made of oak apart from the veneering on the front. The brass handles, knobs, and key-hole escutcheon are all original. The swan-neck handles suggest a later rather than earlier date, but the piece is eminently representative of the Queen Anne period. It may be noted that the bracket feet are a feature of the 18th century, as opposed to bun feet which were typically William and Mary.

Fig 21 is an unusual walnut chest of drawers, again of exceptional charm, showing perhaps more Dutch influence than usual. The shaped drawer fronts in bow form would have been very complex to make and called for a high degree of craftsmanship. Again the finest veneer has been chosen for the drawer fronts and top, while interesting mouldings catch the light admirably on the top, around the base, and between the drawers.

Fig 22 shows a walnut bachelor's chest – a shallow chest of drawers which has a fold-over top, supported by pull-out lopers or bearers. This form of furniture is traditionally thought to have been used by a bachelor for dressing, writing, powdering his wig, indeed for all his requirements. I doubt, in fact, that these pieces were made solely for such specific purposes. This one is an exceptionally fine colour and the arrangement of the drawers is unusual. More frequently there are two short drawers at the top and long drawers below. The fold-over top has a fine moulding around each half-section, arranged in such a way that the two will fit together tightly when the top is folded forwards. The original brass handles, being ring handles with back plates, show a somewhat backward-looking characteristic of the 17th century. The large key escutcheons charge the piece with added character. In the veneering of the drawers you can see how panels of burr wood are framed within cross-bandings of straight veneers, and between the two are laid thinner bands of veneer in herring-bone fashion, that is, two fine bands laid diagonally. This was a common form of ornament in walnut veneering.

The walnut knee-hole desk in fig 23 is especially interesting in that it bears the trade label of the maker or retailer, Elizabeth Bell. It is inscribed 'At the White Swan against the South Gate in St Paul's churchyard, London'. Made in about 1720, this little desk is also a wonderful, faded, warm colour. The trade label is in a small, almost secret, drawer below the long top drawer and fitted above a small cupboard which is in the knee-hole. In this case, burr veneers have been chosen for the top of the desk while well figured but less varied wood has been used on the drawer fronts, on the door, and on the sides. Interesting brasswork, again the original, gives the piece added richness. In this case, the handles and key escutcheons are combined in one piece. The desk stands on bracket feet. Other, slightly larger, knee-hole desks often have additional feet on either side of the knee-hole in front. Sometimes a top drawer pulls out to reveal a fitted interior, the front of the drawer folding down to form part of the writing section. In others the top of the knee-hole desk will fold open to reveal compartments, probably used for dressing. There might be a mirror, on a folding support, and spaces for pin cushions and other dressing or writing requirements.

The reading table or architecture table, illustrated in fig 24, is a more unusual piece of early 18th-century furniture. Its ratcheted fold-up top will support a large book while the pull-out section in the base of the table also has a folding support for a manuscript or book and the surface is lined with black leather. Small, round, swivelling shelves to support candles fold into the sides of the table, and a large brass handle on the front is strong enough to support the full weight of the table when it is pulled forward, as well as being a highly decorative feature. When closed, the front legs of the writing section fold neatly into the canted front legs of the main framework and the inner sides of all the legs are carved with a quarter column pilaster in order to add lightness to the design.

Fig 25 shows a walnut tall-boy of splendid proportions and a fine light colour. It is entirely characteristic of the best walnut furniture of the first quarter of the 18th century. The top half is perfectly in proportion with the lower half. The cornice at the top is echoed by the mouldings around the middle, where the two parts are entirely separate, and with the base where bracket feet support the entire cabinet. The sizes and arrangement of drawers are well-proportioned, and the whole piece is richly ornamented with fine quality pierced brass handles. Lightening the overall design and adding an extra refinement are the carved pilaster mouldings on the front corners of the upper section.

Another cabinet, fig 26 is a walnut bookcase with glazed doors containing bevelled glass plates. The proportions of this bookcase are characteristic of the period. It has a drop waist, with shelves coming down lower than was usual later in the century. This design is reminiscent of the famous oak bookcases made for Samuel Pepys in the 17th century. Georgian bookcases usually had drawers or cupboards in the lower section made to waist height.

Fig 27 shows a charming small bureau on a stand supported by cabriole legs. This piece dates from the reign of George I and is rather more richly decorated, having shaped toes almost in the form of claw feet, and shells carved in the knees. When walnut was plentiful, large cabinets including full-size bureau bookcases were common. At the same time there was a demand for small pieces of furniture like this one, and, from time to time, we see

24 An early 18th-century architect's table, practical but expensively made
with fine walnut veneers, cross bandings and useful fitments.

narrow bureau bookcases made on a diminutive scale, which must have been suited to relatively small rooms.

Fig 28 is a very elegant walnut side-table of simple lines with little decoration. The concave sides are not even ornamented with handles, although in tables such as this there is often a concealed drawer. The dainty cabriole legs end in simple pad feet. In this case proportions, line, and colour say it all.

Fig 29 is another restrained side-table, supported by cabriole legs standing on 'Spanish' toes. It has three drawers, two deep with a shallow one between suggesting that the piece might have been suitable as a dressing or writing table. The delightful colour and patination of the veneers is especially notable. In walnut furniture there can be many variations in colour. Such differences are very much a matter of personal taste. Muddy, dark, boring veneers can never be attractive but in fine-quality pieces there is a great variety of lighter, plainer, burr or heavily marked woods, some of which might appeal to one person while others will choose something else.

25 (left) An early 18th-century tallboy, walnut-veneered on oak and pine with graded drawers.

26 (right) A bookcase of the same materials with glazed doors, a slide and drawers below.

The small centre table of fig 30 has delightful proportions and is a charming nutty colour. The angled, gently cabriole legs with slightly accentuated, outward pointing feet terminating in diamond toes add to its charm, as does the gently curved frieze and the mouldings around the top. At the corners of the top the moulding follows a shape sometimes referred to as the baby's bottom motif. It is frequently used on table and chest tops.

27-30 Four charming and typical Queen Anne period walnut pieces, each fulfilling slightly different domestic requirements.

Fig 31 shows another walnut side table, this time with a decorative feature adopted from Dutch furniture – a sunburst motif in parquetry, set in a small apse at the centre of the piece. This table has many other admirable features including a clear definition between the cabriole legs and the upper corner sections of the framework.

Fig 32 is an especially fine and charming card table of walnut with 'parcel gilt' – or partially gilt – mouldings. The carved mouldings and decoration on the knees and feet are coated with gesso and gilded to give richness to the piece. The table is pictured open to reveal four roundels at the corners where candlesticks could be placed. The fold-back top is supported by two legs which pull out on a concertina action framework. In some cases a single leg only swings back on an arm to support the folding top; but the advantage of two legs in a concertina action is that when the table is open it has a supporting apron around all sides which of course improves its appearance.

31 A walnut-veneered side table with cabriole legs, and with a sunburst motif on the central drawer front (circa 1710).

Fig 33 shows a group of early 18th-century furniture including a walnut knee-hole desk supported on four bracket feet and some gilt pieces. I shall say more about giltwood furniture shortly but, like the card table (fig 32), the torchères on either side of the knee-hole desk and the mirror above are decorated in carved gesso then gilded, a technique much used in rich circles in this period. The rounded form of the torchères reflects some characteristics of the 17th century, but there is an added elegance and restrained gracefulness of line. The ornamentation is limited to relatively superficial bas relief carving. The mirror above also has simple linear mouldings and shallow carved decoration.

Early 18th-century chairs are especially fascinating. In contrast to the elaborate, formal yet flamboyant carved oak and walnut chairs of the 17th century we now see simpler, cleaner lines where the emphasis is not so much on carving, as on veneering over an elegant framework of oak or beech. The

32 (left) A fold-over card table of walnut with parcel-gilt mouldings.

33 A group of early 18th-century furniture showing a walnut knee-hole desk, a pair of carved gesso and gilt torchères and a looking-glass of the same technique.

fine colour of walnut veneers was displayed on flat surfaces as far as possible. Gradually, carved ornament was added to enrich legs and backs. First however, plain cabriole legs, splat backs with curved supports, and square or shaped seat frames were the principal elements of chair design. Mallett's has had many fine examples from this early period. One of the finest is a set of chairs, formerly at Campsey Ash, made around 1720 (fig 34). These chairs display an outstanding elegance of design and incorporate many of the best features of the period, being of a superb colour, with a certain amount of fine carving, and above all standing well. The flat surfaces of the backs, the central splats around the seat frames, and the solid carved legs all show well-coloured walnut while the carved elements, which have been gilt, lift the chairs to a degree of importance without ostentation. Furthermore, the drop-in upholstered seats of the chairs are covered with very fine needlework of the period, though not original. Comfortable upholstered chairs continued as a luxury from the late 17th century, and there are a number of fine Queen

34 A superbly proportioned pair of walnut side chairs with carved and gilded enrichments, from Campsey Ash, Suffolk (circa 1720).

Anne wing armchairs some still retaining their original needlework coverings. A good example is illustrated in fig 35. This has needlework on all the sides except the back (which never had needlework). The embroidery is consistent with the shape of the chair, in this case with flowers mirrored on the outsides and insides of the wings. Similarly there is usually a unity of design in the back and the seat of the chair.

An unusual and rare survival of the period is the cock-fighting chair in fig 36. This chair, which may equally have been made for a library, could be used for sitting in either direction, enabling the user to watch a fighting cock and make notes, or to read a book. The arms contain small fold-out drawers fitted with compartments for inkwells. In the front of the seat of the chair is a shallow drawer. The solid walnut legs are delicately carved in light relief and the chair retains its original leather.

Another kind of armchair associated with these times is a more feminine upholstered armchair of light design. Fig 37 shows a shepherd's crook

35 (left) A Queen Anne wing chair or easy chair retaining its original splendid needlework executed in wools highlighted with some silk.

36 (right) A walnut cockfighting chair upholstered with leather. It is possible to sit in this chair facing in either direction.

37 *A walnut 'shepherd's crook' armchair retaining its original needlework.*

38 *A pair of walnut side chairs, circa 1725, with elements of carving and drop-in needlework seats.*

armchair of about 1710, so called because of the crook-like shape of the arms. The escutcheon back is covered with contemporary needlework, as is the seat, and the straight legs with pad toes are joined with elegant stretchers.

As the walnut period progressed into the reigns of George I and George II, there was a trend towards more ornamentation. Fig 38 shows a pair of walnut side-chairs where the characteristic cabriole legs and shaped splat-backs are retained, but where the design is a good deal heavier and charged with rich ornamental carving. Notice the ball and claw toes, the shell motif on the front seat rail, the carving on the knees, the fine work on the cresting of the chair and on the back splat, together with the accentuated shaping of the chair backs, which all contribute to a greater sense of richness fashionable by the mid 1720s.

Fig 39 shows two of a set of eight chairs where again there is a restrained but rich combination of veneering and carving. Stretchers between the legs are back in fashion giving physical support and weight to the design. The knees and feet of the chairs are especially well carved with acanthus leaves, and there is fine work on the cresting. Furthermore, the seats of this set retain extremely fine needlework coverings of circa 1720. Each seat is different in design and yet all are linked in colour and feeling.

The ultimate in walnut chairs for elaborate shape and carving is represented by a pair of chairs in fig 41. These highly decorative, even eccentric, chairs show an originality and caricature design which is hard to beat. The rococo legs are somewhat exaggerated while the shaped backs are wonderfully fanciful and richly carved. The crestings are surmounted by Chinese pagodas and the seat frames are faced by Chinese trellis. These and other details are picked out in parcel gilding to give contrast to the polished walnut, both solid elements and veneered parts. The seats of these chairs are also upholstered in fine contemporary needlework.

Fig 40 illustrates one of a pair of elegant walnut stools upholstered with very good needlework of the period. These stools have a simple line with modest pad toes, but are enriched with shell motifs carved on the knees. Another charming stool of small proportions is strengthened by an elegant cross stretcher decorated with a central carved leaf (fig 42).

Of the many fine walnut bureau bookcases which Mallett's has been fortunate to handle, one I have always admired is (fig 43) attributed to Giles Grendy. This grand piece, made in about 1725, is of richly coloured walnut on an oak carcass, enriched by gilt gesso mouldings, and bearing fine gilt brass handles and mounts on the bombé shaped base. The ogee-shaped bracket feet and the broken classical swan-neck pediment, enclosing a giltwood cartouche and supported by finials, give the piece a splendid status

39 (left) Two of a set of walnut side chairs, magnificently veneered and carved, and retaining fine needlework seats, circa 1720.

40 (below) An elegant walnut stool, circa 1710.

42 (above) Another Queen Anne stool, of oval form and with the legs joined by stretchers.

41 (left) This exuberant pair of side chairs (circa 1740) shows the continued use of walnut at a time when mahogany was more fashionable. The complex wood work is decorated with carving, and some parts are gilded.

43 In contrast to the smaller pieces of walnut furniture, domestic in nature, is this magnificent bureau bookcase made in about 1725, with a broken pediment, shaped mirror doors, a bombé base, water-gilt mouldings and gilt brass mounts.

and grandeur, characteristic of the George I period. This is a large piece of furniture but it is interesting to note that smaller cabinets were also made with the same degree of importance and elaborateness. Indeed, Mallett's has also had a piece of furniture almost identical to this bureau in every detail except that it was narrower, smaller, and had a single mirror door instead of a pair (fig 44).

Possibly unique is a huge walnut bookcase which once belonged to Admiral Rodney, a contemporary of Lord Nelson. This colossal piece (fig 46) has several unusual features. Dating from around 1720-25, it is a conventional bureau bookcase in many respects but, instead of a fall-front writing section, there are two opening doors and a pull-out section on which to write. The piece is fitted with cupboards and columns containing secret drawers in the base as well as within the interior of the writing section. The top is also similarly fitted with pigeon-holes and compartments.

Fig 45 shows a modestly scaled but very fine cabinet of narrow proportions but superbly made and fitted in the interior with compartments for documents.

One of the most remarkable pieces of furniture we have had was a very rare early 18th-century gilt gesso bureau cabinet (fig 47) in the manner of James

44 and 45 Two walnut bureau bookcases of narrow proportions, and each with a single door in the upper section. Fig 45 (right) shows elaborate interior compartments.

Moore who supplied furniture to the royal family. Conventionally proportioned and designed, the piece is uniquely decorated on the exterior with gilt carved gesso. It is believed that the bookcase was one of a pair given by Queen Anne to the King of Portugal. The second piece was known as recently as 1940 but sadly was lost in war damage. Our cabinet was not known until it appeared in the sale-rooms in 1977. It was disguised under a cloak of 19th-century ornament, with much of the original gilt decoration hidden beneath layers of later oil gilding. Mallett's realised the importance of the cabinet and was able to restore it to its original glory preserving much of

46 The Rodney cabinet, an unusually grand bureau bookcase with several panels of mirror, and with the unusual feature of folding doors enclosing the writing section and a slide instead of a fall front.

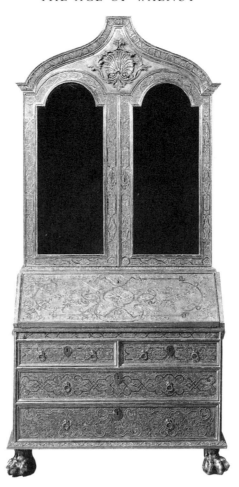

the original gilding. Happily, it was thereby identified, rescued, and saved for posterity.

By the third and fourth decades of the 18th century walnut played a less prominent part in the story of furniture making; it was used less for its fine colour but remained an excellent wood for carving in rich detail. There were new demands for richness, for more important and grandiose interiors. Fig 48 shows a walnut side-table with a marble top. It exemplifies superb carving in its flowing acanthus leaves, a central basket of flowers, and the confident claw and ball feet. The carving is gilded; only the legs show the natural colour of the wood. This splendid table stands nobly, proud and unapologetic, displaying wealth and confidence. This was the growing trend after the first quarter of the 18th century. Another delightful pair of objects, more reminiscent of the late 17th century, is shown in fig 49. These rare table globes, one celestial, the other terrestrial, are made by Charles Price, and one is dated 1714. They stand 19½in high, and demonstrate the increasing interest in the world of science and natural history, anticipating the prolific manufacture of globes when this became fashionable in the late 18th and early 19th centuries. The maker's label on one of the globes gives Charles Price's address and he proudly describes himself as 'Hydrographer to the King'.

47 A remarkable and probably unique walnut-lined bureau bookcase entirely decorated on the outside with carved and gilt gesso, circa 1710.

48 A noble carved walnut side-table of about 1740, bearing a slab marble top and with the classical and floreate carving emphasised with gilding.

49 (below) A pair of table globes by Charles Price, one dated 1714.

54

LACQUER

*T*here is a surprising amount of lacquer furniture in Europe, especially in England. From the 17th century onwards, like other oriental imports highly prized for their exotic, novel, and decorative features, lacquer was imported in considerable amounts and was included in most great houses. It was not so much that it was precious, but it had curiosity value and was the latest fashion. Lacquer today is seen in various different forms on furniture, each very distinctive. They may be summarised as follows:

First, Chinese lacquer furniture was imported in the 17th, 18th and 19th centuries. These pieces have not been altered in any way except perhaps given a base to raise them to the height of normal European furniture. Screens and cabinets were particularly popular in the earlier period but by the second half of the 18th century other articles, such as knee-hole desks and even large bureau bookcases, of European shape, were specially produced in China for export.

Secondly, Japanese furniture of a similar nature was brought in, especially cabinets in the 19th century. These also were not altered substantially. In addition we see many smaller Japanese lacquer objects such as boxes.

50 Detail of a late 17th-century Chinese coromandel lacquer screen of a kind that was frequently imported to Europe.

Thirdly, panels of Chinese and Japanese lacquer were imported to Europe and cut up in order to be used in making French and English furniture or for wall panels. This probably included complete screens.

Lastly, we see European imitations of Chinese and Japanese lacquer, as well as much that does not resemble either closely but is clearly based on the general appearance of the medium. This is known as japanning.

Travellers and merchants in the 17th century quickly discovered that there was a strong market for oriental wares in Europe, particularly for lacquer screens from China. Several varieties of lacquer were imported but one of the earliest and best known was 'coromandel', which was first brought overland to the Coromandel coast in India where it was collected by English merchants who shipped it to Europe. This lacquer was very beautiful and was much favoured in Europe.

Large screens, often of 12 folding panels, were decorated on one or both sides on a black, brown, or plum coloured background (fig 50). The principal designs consisted of complex decoration in polychromes incised into the polished dark ground. The best screens often have a courtly landscape on one side, with walls and courtyards, sometimes with many figures going about various pursuits, while on the other side there would be a garden scene with rocks, a wonderful variety of flowering shrubs and plants, and flying simurg birds in male and female forms, some with peacock-like feathers. Both sides of the screen are usually within borders depicting smaller scenes or various auspicious objects. Some screens have only one decorative side while the back is engraved or inscribed with columns of panegyric addressed to a Chinese nobleman. These inscriptions can often be translated but are usually found to be somewhat altered for various reasons.

This type of incised coromandel lacquer was the first to be cut up and used in making furniture; it is frequently seen incorporated in French or English commodes, and in mirrors, side-tables, and cupboards. Little respect was paid to the narrative scene depicted in the lacquer. Indeed small pieces are often incorporated at angles, on their sides, or upside down in patchwork formation. A magnificent cushion mirror at Boughton House, Northamptonshire, for example, shows two sides of the mirror veneered with pieces of coromandel lacquer on their sides. Another mirror, similarly treated, can be seen at Ham House, Surrey.

I have already shown how lacquer chests were imported in the 17th century and were mounted on giltwood or silvered bases, sometimes with a cresting

above (see fig 7). A rare example of a Chinese coromandel cabinet being given such treatment is shown in fig 52. In this case there is no cresting; there may or may not have been one originally, but the giltwood base is very fine and was made in England in about 1670. Blue and white oriental porcelain was quite frequently used in conjunction with lacquer in English houses and it may well have been that a garniture of vases was placed on the top of a non-crested cabinet such as this.

From this time on, japanning was extremely popular in England, and a considerable amount of very fine and important furniture with English 'lacquer' decoration has survived. It was done in several background colours, usually with gilt chinoiserie motifs superimposed. The principle colours were red, green, blue and black, although white was used occasionally. Lacquer decoration might be applied to any furniture of European form; it did not seem incongruous to decorate such furniture with oriental-style motifs – just as it was fashionable to incorporate 'Indian' embroideries or woven silks into European dress. The once serious iconography of oriental ornament became fully adopted into European culture as a purely decorative feature. Indeed fashions today of chintz curtains and 'oriental' vases continue this disregard

51 Oriental lacquer screens and panels were frequently cut up to be used
for decorating English and other European furniture.

52 A 17th-century Chinese coromandel lacquer cabinet brought to
Europe and displayed on a fine carved giltwood Charles II stand.

for the original symbolic meaning of some of the subject matter. Many of the floral patterns on fabrics which appear to be inspired by English gardens are in fact derived from Chinese originals. Most familiar of all are the chinoiserie motifs on our day to day crockery, transposed from the original imported 'china'.

A William and Mary side-table with a dressing mirror on it (fig 53), made in England around 1690, is entirely decorated with green japanning. The mirror retains its original plate with an engraved star, and the table legs are joined by a stretcher with a small plinth which could support an oriental vase. The mirror has a small bureau section; below this is a drawer which is fitted with compartments and still contains some original fittings including boxes and a brush.

Another dressing table mirror of slightly later date (fig 54) is decorated like porcelain with reserves of white lacquer painted in polychrome, and framed in black lacquer enriched with gold chinoiserie trelliswork. Small boxes, a pin cushion and a little brush still survive in the drawer of this piece.

The grandest of all japanned furniture in England were bureau bookcases and secretaire cabinets; Mallett's has specialised in these over the years. I

53 A William and Mary side-table with a toilet mirror en suite, both decorated with English green lacquer or japanning.

54 (right) A japanned dressing table mirror with boxes that fit into the drawer.

shall illustrate a few of the outstanding examples we have had. The largest, and perhaps the noblest, was one in red lacquer, said to have been made in England for the Spanish market (fig 55). It was later taken to Italy and was once in the Pope's summer apartments at the Quirinale Palace. Instead of the more conventional arrangement of compartments and pigeon-holes, its noble proportions contain a large number of small, regular drawers all decorated with gold chinoiseries. This scarlet lacquer was very much to the taste of European patrons. But the bright colours seen in England were not derived from furniture imported from the Far East, which was invariably dark, usually black. Only the chinoiserie decoration was truly oriental.

Fig 56 shows a splendid green lacquer double-domed bureau bookcase. Here the interior is fitted with a variety of drawers, document compartments, small cupboards, and, behind pilasters, secret drawers. Fig 57 shows a black lacquer bureau bookcase with a broken pediment and with the mirror doors that were so much a feature of the finest and most extravagant lacquer furniture supplied in the early part of the 18th century.

As with walnut furniture, lacquer bureau bookcases were sometimes very small with an almost jewel-like character. One of the most remarkable is illustrated in fig 58. With a small single door, and mirror fronted, the cabinet is richly decorated with scarlet japanning and gold chinoiseries. The top is surmounted with a gilt gesso cresting while the base is in bombé form and stands on gilt claw and ball feet. Another interesting feature is the folding brushing slide above the three long drawers. The overall height is 6ft 1½in.

Another very remarkable black lacquer bureau bookcase (fig 59) is dated slightly later, circa 1725. It may be compared with the walnut bureau bookcase illustrated in fig 43 as it has many similar features, but this one is decorated overall in very elaborate gilt chinoiseries on a black ground. It has a classical broken pediment and the gilt metal handles on the drawers are of the finest quality.

The red lacquer knee-hole desk in fig 60 is an exceedingly rare item and may be German rather than English. This possibly unique piece is a superb colour and the chinoiseries are worked in different tones of gold. It is fitted with a fall-front drawer containing a writing compartment but otherwise its form is comparable to the walnut knee-hole discussed on page 37.

Chairs were also given japanned decoration. The beech frames might be decorated in various colours. In the 17th century they were invariably black with a small amount of bright coloured decoration, but, in the early 18th century, red, green, black, blue, or occasionally white were also known. A magnificent pair of William and Mary black japanned armchairs have already been discussed (see fig 10). Another charming pair of chairs with coloured decoration on a white ground is shown in fig 62.

55 A most unusual large-scale red lacquer bureau bookcase from the Pope's summer apartments at the Quirinale Palace. The brilliant red exterior and many small drawers inside are richly decorated with gold chinoiseries. The cabinet is enclosed by mirrored doors.

56 A Queen Anne green lacquer bureau bookcase of double dome format and with numerous compartments, including secret drawers behind the pilasters.

57 (right) A black japanned bureau bookcase with an arched broken pediment.

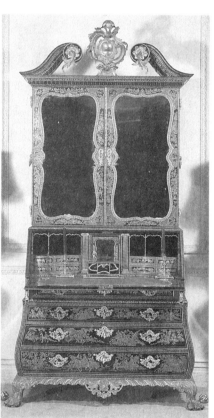

58 (right) An exceptional small-sized bureau cabinet of scarlet lacquer
with giltwood enrichments, the upper section enclosed by a single mirror-
fronted door, circa 1720.

59 (left) A richly decorated black lacquer bureau bookcase.

Japanning was not only done on woodwork, it was also applied to metal. Tole jardinières, wine cisterns, coolers and other objects are found with fine lacquer decoration, frequently incorporating chinoiseries on a coloured or black ground. The tole tea-kettle (fig 61) has comfortable English proportions on which the decoration is red charged with gilt chinoiseries.

Clocks have always been greatly prized. Three fine examples of long-case clocks with japanned cases are illustrated in fig 63. All have good movements, though none is by the most famous London makers. Lacquer was not used for the most important timepieces; it was a specialised decorative

60 (opposite above) This most unusual scarlet lacquer knee-hole desk, with fallfront writing drawer, is possibly German though very much of an English form. The chinoiserie decoration, which includes European figures, is in gold with black details and some of the motifs are raised on a gesso foundation. Circa 1715.

61 (opposite below) Relatively humble tôle objects for domestic use, such as this kettle, were sometimes given japanned decoration.

62 (above) A highly decorative pair of early 18th-century side chairs, with caned backs and seats, are decorated in the rarest colour, white with polychrome patterns.

63 Three very decorative 18th-century long case clocks, each treated differently. The first is in black and gold lacquer; the second, like porcelain, has reserves filled with polychrome chinoiseries; and the third has unusual still-life panels within 'oriental' borders.

art for those with a taste for the unusual. Fig 64 shows a charming red lacquer bracket clock of about 1720. A good number of these survive but relatively few in very good condition. Frequently, the lacquer decoration has deteriorated, and even more often it has been badly restored – so much so that much of the charm as well as the originality has disappeared.

We have already seen some imported Chinese furniture in its original form, unaltered except, perhaps, for a base to stand on. In addition to cabinets, lacquer blanket chests can frequently be seen in the great English houses. A very fine black lacquer chest of about 1740, fig 65, has been given an English giltwood stand of around the same date. The stand is in the form of two dragons (no doubt thought to be emblematic of China but, in fact, very un-Chinese in character) and supports a framework with Vitruvian scrolls with a double shell motif at the centre. Many similar chests survive but seldom with such a fine stand as this.

The 'look-alike' Chinese character of this English base for a genuine oriental chest brings us to the essence of chinoiserie – Europeans created what they considered was an amusing, oriental imitation to conform with Georgian decoration. In developing this Europeans did not necessarily wish to ape Chinese furniture but wanted to create something exotic, described by the general term 'Indian'. The Gothic chairs illustrated in fig 66, for example,

64 A fine early 18th-century bracket clock by William Smith of London is given a charming red lacquer case.

are decorated with black and gold, while the woodwork is in a most fascinating, bizarre form – a wonderful conception of mid-18th-century fantasy. These two chairs are part of a set of four which came from Stonor Park, Oxfordshire.

The remarkable and most original set of George III chairs in fig 67 consists of six side-chairs and one armchair. They are decorated in black with fine gold flowers on the hooped members of the back, arms, and feet rails. Beechwood frames in this design would normally be very frail so the chair-maker has used a form of lamination to give strength to his woodwork. This set of chairs has only a general mood of chinoiserie in the overall effect of frivolity and in the back decoration, which is black with gold flowers laid over it.

A magnificent pair of large English commodes (fig 68) was formerly at Uppark, West Sussex, where a similar pair remains. Of circa 1765, these commodes are decorated on the door fronts with panels of 18th-century Chinese lacquer, probably cut from a screen. The tops also incorporate smaller pieces of genuine Chinese lacquer. The other mouldings and borders are entirely English with chinoiserie decoration. The French-inspired serpentine form is complemented with gilt mounts on the front corners and gilt scrolls on the front legs. Whereas in French furniture, and in certain English pieces, these mounts would have been ormolu (gilded bronze), in this

65 A Chinese black lacquer coffer is here transformed into a piece of furniture by the addition of an English giltwood stand in the Chinese manner (circa 1740).

66 and 67 Mid 18th-century fantasy and romanticism are captured in these gothic armchairs (above), which have japanned decoration as do the contemporary hoop-backed chairs below.

68 and 69 One of a set of four magnificent commodes, above, two of
which are still at Uppark, West Sussex. Panels of Chinese lacquer have
been incorporated in the design of great English furniture, circa 1765.
Another noteworthy example is a commode from Harewood House,
Yorkshire, attributed to Thomas Chippendale, below.

case the enrichments are entirely of carved wood, gilded. This is an unusual and especially charming feature. The scale is quite large; each commode is 4ft 10in wide.

A particularly magnificent commode, circa 1775 (fig 69), is similarly English but partly made with panels of Chinese black and gold lacquer. This important piece is fitted on the inside with drawers which have superb floral japanned fronts. The commode came from Harewood House, Yorkshire, and is attributed to Thomas Chippendale, possibly after a design by Robert Adam.

Another charming commode, of smaller proportions and delicate flowing lines (fig 70), is one of a pair which we had at different times. This piece belonged to the late Duke of Kent. Like the Uppark pair, it incorporates oriental lacquer in an English commode of French inspiration. The mounts on the corners are, however, ormolu.

70 Another smaller but elegant commode in the French taste has true oriental lacquer fitted to the curved doors (circa 1770).

From a later period – the early 19th century – is a splendid Japanese lacquer cabinet together with its original stand made for the European market (fig 71). Like a wonderfully embroidered Japanese kimono this piece is ravishingly decorated with flowers and partridges.

Another cabinet, made in Japan around 1800 or soon after, is shown in fig 72. The outside is of tortoiseshell coloured lacquer, with panels depicting rocks and flowers. The interior, however, displays superb falcons on the back of the doors, while the drawer fronts within are decorated with tortoiseshell lacquer overlaid with loose feathers. The drawer handles and locks are gilded metal. A later Japanese cabinet (fig 73) is of black and gold lacquer, inset with panels of porcelain in the drawer fronts and sliding doors. The cabinet is placed on a stand similarly decorated, part of the original conception.

71 An early 19th-century Japanese lacquer cabinet on a stand, richly decorated with partridges in an abundant garden.

72 The interior of a magnificent Japanese cabinet made for the European market, decorated with hawks, textiles and feathers on a tortoiseshell background.

73 (below, left) and 74 (below, right) Another Japanese cabinet incorporating porcelain panels; and a magnificent Japanese chest displaying Mount Fuji and a boat, on an English stand.

A magnificent coffer (fig 75) made in the Far East, probably for a local patron, is in a classic antiquarian form, having a traditional bronze treasure chest appearance. It is thought to date from the 17th century; the plum colour lacquer is profusely inlaid with pieces of mother of pearl in delicate interlocking rosettes. The chest is further ornamented with gilded metal mounts, corners, feet, and other bandings where protection is needed.

A magnificent sixfold screen (fig 76), in black lacquer with large red panels decorated with gilding, is of Chinese origin and depicts English or Portuguese travellers to the Far East in various activities. Western and oriental figures can be seen riding in sedan chairs, hunting, visiting palaces, and taking part in dragon festivities. The Europeans' costumes and full-bottomed wigs are clearly described.

In the second half of the 18th century, the Chinese made a considerable quantity of furniture to meet European requirements. While the form of this furniture is almost indistinguishable from European pieces, the construction and decoration are very different. The cabinet making is usually rather naive. Joints are crude and the wood of relatively poor quality. The decoration, usually black and gold only, is, however, of fine workmanship – hard and crisp. Figs 77 and 78 show furniture made in China for the European market. The first shows a knee-hole desk, the second a pair of tall cabinets with curious inward bowed bases and interestingly shaped pediment tops. Oriental furniture is often decorated on all sides, and, in the case of this pair of cabinets, where the top sections lift off the lower sections, even the inner sides have gilt decoration.

75 (above) A splendid lacquer coffer of antiquarian form, the plum coloured lacquer profusely inlaid with mother-of-pearl. Circa 1690.

76 (opposite, above) A fascinating red and black screen, showing European figures at various pursuits, circa 1710.

77 and 78 (opposite, below, left and right) A Chinese black lacquer knee-hole desk made for the European market; and one of an exotic pair of Chinese cabinets made for export to England, circa 1780.

GILTWOOD

*S*olid silver had been used in exceptional cases for furniture making in the reigns of Charles I and Charles II. A few pieces survive at Windsor Castle and at Knole in Kent, while smaller objects, such as silver wall lights, have survived in some numbers. These are very magnificent of course, but greater flexibility of design, and in some ways even greater richness, could be achieved by gilding wood. Carved wood, gilded and highly burnished or with various different patterns, textures, and matt effects, could give an effect of solid gold, and make a brilliant impact. Side-tables with pier glasses above them, sets of chairs and stools, picture frames around portraits and old master paintings, and every other variety of furniture, could be given the appearance of true gold metal in a splendour that is almost inconceivable. Nowadays, of course, we see a very much toned-down, mellowed, worn gilding and this seems to us fully representative of earlier richness. But when this furniture was originally made, it was very much brighter and often had a truly metallic look belying the wooden framework underneath.

A way to experience something of the rich, Midas-like appearance of many great apartments of the past is to visit antique restoration workshops where gilding is being done on a large scale. There, a glance around a room may include side-tables, mirror-frames, and sets of chairs in a partially finished, burnished but untoned state, just as giltwood furniture must have looked

79 One of a magnificent pair of early 18th-century mirrors showing inspiration from the French but distinctly English and bearing the Tyrrell family crest. The simplicity of line is augmented by bevelled glass plates and borders.

when new. In antique restoration some rubbing through must be done, not only to tone in with other antique furniture, but because the untoned brightness of newly laid gold, without history's patination or a sympathetic helping hand, appears garish and is not appealing to modern taste.

One of the greatest luxuries in 17th- and 18th-century houses was mirror glass, and plates of this material were invariably given special frames in order to celebrate them and show them off. At Hampton Court Palace, some of the magnificent, large pier glasses between the windows have fine bevelled glass frames with very little or no woodwork in view. Many smaller early mirrors also had relatively slight frames but included interestingly shaped mirror glass borders with bevelled facets. Fig 80 shows a fine William and Mary mirror of this kind, with a simple woodwork frame supporting the main and bordering plates. As mentioned before (page 28), decorated glass known as verre eglomisé was sometimes used in a similar manner. The mirror illustrated, being 'landscape' in form, was made to go above a fireplace and is especially elegant. The limited, carved wood decoration on the corners and at the top is conceived to give the appearance of embossed metal mounts.

A magnificent pair of early 18th-century mirrors (fig 79) from Littlecote,

80 A William and Mary overmantel mirror with bevelled and decorated plates enclosed within a glass and carved giltwood border.

81 (opposite) A magnificent pier glass, circa 1700, incorporating large mirror plates, with a bevelled mirror border surmounted by an elaborate giltwood cresting of strapwork.

Berkshire, have glass borders and mirror crestings, all with carved giltwood frames and enrichments, supporting the crests of the Tyrrell family at the top. These mirrors have a feeling of the French Regence but are certainly English. The scale is large (7ft 5in high) but, although noble in proportion and design, they still have a calmness and elegance typical of that felicitous combination of Huguenot and English craftsmanship.

Fig 81 shows another especially fine late 17th-century pier glass which must once have had a suitably weighty table beneath it in order to complete the design. The mirror has the traditional two large plates as big as it was possible to make, and the upper one is decorated with bevelled ferns. The mirror is framed within a border of glass and the joints of the pieces are disguised with panels of lightly carved wood. Around the top of the mirror is a superb cresting of carved giltwood in the form of scrolls and curling foliage. One longs to discover the provenance of such magnificent pieces as this, but we only know that it once belonged to the late Countess of Portarlington.

Before leaving furniture related to the 17th century I must point out a very concise and delightful pair of giltwood wall brackets (fig 82), which in many ways echo the more expensive silver versions of the period. These two giltwood sconces bear the Earl of Radnor's crest and coronet at the top. The richness of ideas and delicacy of the carving, where fluidity is combined with serious ornament, make these small treasures of the period.

As mentioned already, the Queen Anne period saw a greater simplicity of line and ornament than the William and Mary period at the end of the 17th century. By the early 1700s we see a simplicity and flow in line of extreme sophistication. The magnificent chair illustrated in fig 84 is justly celebrated, although its origin is unknown. The chair is larger than might be expected and must have been part of a very noble set which may have included armchairs and stools. The elegant, gentle cabriole legs ending in squared diamond toes, the detailing of the mouldings, the carving on the knee, and the light scrolling at the back of the chair, the sides, and at the cresting, are all full of grace. The chair may have been upholstered with velvet or perhaps with a rich woven silk. In any event it must clearly have been covered with a rich, costly material. A comparable chair in the Victoria and Albert Museum is upholstered with red and gold cut velvet of the period.

A fine oval mirror (fig 83) displays a similar simplicity of design with nothing to compete with its delightfully restrained, though extremely costly, oval glass plate which has curved bevelling forming an inner frame. The simple cresting of acanthus leaves with a huge shell is poised delicately above. The shell motif is a typical emblem of the period.

82 (opposite, left above) A pair of 17th-century candle sconces.

83 (opposite, left below) An early 18th-century oval mirror with glass border.

84 (opposite, right) A large giltwood side chair of exceptional elegance and poise, decorated only with discreet carved scrollings.

Another mirror (fig 85) has a curious combination of early 18th-century motifs. The frame is again enclosed within glass borders, partly in the form of pilasters with giltwood Corinthian capitals above and supporting finials. There is a shell at the base between two brass sconces for candles which would reflect light into the room. The cresting of the mirror is in the form of a broken pediment enclosing a cartouche of a female head with stylised feathers or leaves in the Indian manner.

Early chandeliers were usually of brass, and silver in special circumstances. A good many brass chandeliers have survived, and happily, some very fine ones can still be seen in the churches and cathedrals where they were originally hung. But fig 86 shows one of a splendid pair which once hung at Holme Lacey, Herefordshire. They are gilded wood with gesso decoration and have gilt lead masks around the main body. The elegant grandeur of these great chandeliers is astonishing, and their appearance in candle-light must certainly have been impressive, with the burnished gold and decoration reflecting the candle flames.

These two chandeliers are largely decorated with the shallow bas relief carving that is familiar on gilt gesso furniture. This restrained form of ornamentation closely follows the strapwork and floral decoration seen in silver, as carried out by Paul de Lamerie and other Huguenot craftsmen. It

85 An early 18th-century looking glass with an unusual glass pilaster border, and a classical pediment containing an Indian mask.

can also be seen on the Queen Anne sofa in fig 87. The design of this item is similar to one that might have been made of figured walnut. It is limited to an elegant curvilinear form, but a sense of richness is achieved in the gilt decoration and in the use of a rich covering fabric.

Another looking-glass, in fig 88, has similar decoration within a frame of gilded gesso. The framework includes pilasters at either side, Corinthian capitals, and a cresting above where the outline partly echoes a broken pediment, with a central cartouche and roundel in the middle. The overhanging, scrolling elements at the top are characteristic of many early 18th-century mirrors, and at the base are the usual fitted brass sconce brackets to hold candles. In this case, the frame has not been re-gilded and the carved gesso retains traces of the original gilding only. This gives a wonderful ivory-gilt effect with great character – a natural and undisturbed state that is rarely seen.

Of a similar nature, but an even rarer survival, is an embroidered needlework picture in a carved gilded gesso frame (fig 89). Both are original to each other and were made in about 1710. The needlework picture is worked in wools highlighted with silks, and depicts a lady and gentleman posing as shepherds in an Arcadian setting. The gilt gesso frame, which measures only 23½in x 17½in, shows on a small scale all the finest elements

86 A large 18th-century gilt gesso chandelier, one of two formerly at Holme Lacey, Herefordshire.

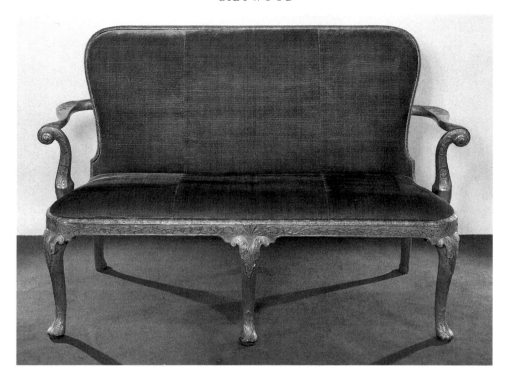

87 and 88 A Queen Anne gilt gesso sofa, circa 1710; and a mirror of the same technique with elegant column sides and scrolling top.

89 (opposite) A remarkable early 18th-century needlework picture, in its original gesso frame with brass candle sconces.

most typical of this type of work. The scrolling acanthus leaves rolling over gadrooned mouldings at the top, the inner picture frame with 'baby's bottom' corners at the top, the scallop shell motif at the base, and the brass sconces are all typical hallmarks of Queen Anne mirror frames, although rarely seen so compactly, and in combination with needlework.

The table shown in fig 90 is one of a pair from Tyttenhanger Park, Hertfordshire, which have simple thin lines yet elegantly support specimen marble tops. The 'broken' cabriole legs have 'Indian' busts at the knees; each mask is crowned with a plume of feathers. The characteristic motif is used here to full effect whereby the half-profile view gives great elegance to the corners of the tables. The rest of the decoration is typical, having shallow carving, pleasantly complex in texture rather than having a sculptured effect. This was a key feature of early 18th-century gilt gesso furniture.

90 *One of a pair of carved gilt side-tables supported by legs with Indian masks and with specimen marble tops.*

91 *This giltwood mirror, one of a pair, shows Queen Anne mirror plates with glass borders re-dressed with the fashionable, more elaborate carving of some thirty years later.*

92 A long gesso side-table, very richly decorated with strapwork masks and scrolling leaves, circa 1720.

The cresting of a pier glass (fig 91) shows the quality of detail and wide variety of textures which could be achieved in carving and gilding gesso, comparable only to the finest work of a silversmith.

The table in fig 92 is an exceptional one in that it is considerably longer and larger than usual. The fineness of the drawing and the carving adds subtlety. Notice the elegant rhythm of the shaped apron along the front of the table. Once again there is a crowned mask in the centre. There are also masks of human faces at the four corners. A few years later, as designs became too heavy and grand to fit into architectural settings, these masks would probably turn into stronger creatures, such as lions' heads, and all the mouldings would become weightier in appearance, even being carved with architectural detail resembling stonework. At the same time the lions' head masks would be echoed with lions' paw feet, and thereafter a whole variety of paws, claws, or claw and ball.

The very grand pair of gilt gesso chairs from Benningborough Hall, Yorkshire (fig 93), are richly charged with ornament, almost over-weighing the elegant, original chair shape with sumptuous gilding. The fairly stiff front legs terminate in monopoid paws totally disproportionate to the heads above. The beautiful backs are elegantly shaped. Worthy of note, too, is the sculptural pattern of the space between the outside of the back and the central splat, as is the overall shape of the chair.

I have already shown how mirror plates were tremendously highly prized, and were frequently given elaborate giltwood frames. Sometimes the same plates would be reframed according to fashion. Fig 94 shows a Queen Anne mirror which has been encased within a very fine giltwood rococo frame of some 20 to 30 years later. Simple mirror plates with faceted mirror borders have been retained and encrusted with the much more elaborate rococo carving that became so fashionable later on. As a result, this pier glass, which is one of a pair, is magically dressed up with grand elements somewhat reminiscent of the designer Mathias Lock, with a scrolling broken pediment flanking a sunburst-type central cartouche. Each mirror is supported by a pair of term busts with chinoiserie leaf hats, and bodies fading into scrolls and flowers, while at the bases there are almost grotesque lions' masks.

The architect William Kent (1686-1748) made a great contribution to furniture design: elements and motifs used in his interiors had an overall unity of design which was carried into most of the allied fields in the decorative arts. As a result, furniture of the 1730s is often more architectural in feeling, more monumental, noble, stationary, and ornate, and seldom whimsical. The motifs reflect a serious grandeur, with pediments, architectural mouldings, columns, pilasters, plinths, large shells or animals such as lions and dolphins. The quiet elegance of the Queen Anne period and gentle ornament of the George I period were replaced by unapologetic, massive, sculptural forms within the context of palladian classicism. This was an age of confidence, of fanfares and social parading.

Eagle console tables, as in fig 95, fitted into the architecture of large white and gilt rooms; the use of marble tops added a further weightiness, suggesting permanence rather than frivolous decoration. These ones were carved from large pieces of pine bonded together by glue. Another pair of tables (fig 96) have elegant inward curving legs; the language of the motifs used in the carved decoration is again reminiscent of William Kent and his followers. The elaborate key pattern around the frieze of the tables, the bearded 'river-god' masks, and heavy swags of flowers beneath them, the scrolling console legs and the grotesque almost fish-like masks on the feet, are all typical emblems of the period.

The double dolphin table in fig 97, supporting a panel of genuine Chinese black lacquer with gold decoration, is a gentler but representative piece of the same period. The dolphins are somewhat plumper and grander than their descendants of the Regency period; there is a splendid scallop shell between their tails and both fish rest on an architectural plinth decorated with the Vitruvian scrolling so much loved by William Kent.

A magnificent pair of stools from Castle Hill, Devon (fig 98), represent the epitome of classical, architectural fantasy condensed into relatively small objects. Here a number of characteristic motifs are linked together with

93 and 94 Gilded furniture must have been wonderfully opulent when it was new. These chairs, of about 1720, are entirely covered with strapwork and carved textures resembling metal work, especially silver. The mirror cresting below is representative of the intricate detailing of such furniture.

incredible richness, incorporating – prominently – elephant masks supported by lions' paw feet, swags and flowers, Vitruvian scrolls, and scallop shells. These stools were conceived as part of a suite of furniture that includes colossal sofas.

In Europe by the 1740s, however, there was a new trend in decoration, frivolous rather than classical. This was 'rococo', with a dancing mass of C-shape scrolls, flowers and all sorts of other motifs, classical, mythological, sculptural, oriental, and gothic thrown in and mixed together in a whimsical pot of fantasy. An Italian carved giltwood console table (fig 99) is a foretaste of the rococo fashions that were to grip England in the wake of continental Europe, and which are so much a central characteristic of what we know today as Chippendale furniture. The chair frame shown in fig 100 still retains a conventional outline, but in each element, especially in the arm, there is a curling, scrolling, and rhythmical ornamentation displaying a new form of joyful luxury.

An outstanding Chippendale period giltwood chandelier (fig 101), from Hornby Castle, the seat of the Duke of Leeds, is attributed to Mathias Lock, circa 1740. An almost identical one attributed to Thomas Chippendale was made for the Earl of Shaftesbury at St Giles House, Dorset. With 15 lights, this splendid rococo *tour de force* is richly carved with swirling leaves and flames, surmounted by an eagle with outstretched wings. The centre section has on it three masks, half hidden behind the riot of asymmetrical details.

As before, mirrors were highly valued and were frequently given expensive frames of carved gilt wood. The variety was enormous, and, in the best and most successful, a great lightness of design was achieved in the rococo period.

95-98 Large bird, animal and fish forms are frequently seen in giltwood furniture of the first half of the 18th century, especially under console tables. The stools above (fig 98) are supported by elephant heads amongst a wealth of classical and baroque ornament.

*99 and 100 Cascading scrolls, busts and masks are combined in an
Italian rococo side-table of about 1750; while similar motifs, though less
prominent, are also a feature of an English giltwood armchair.*

Plates of various shapes and sizes, and sometimes a combination of plates in groups, were given fanciful settings like jewels. Vertical rectangular forms were the most usual. Many variations, however, include a pair of oval mirrors (fig 102), and these often display a general fondness for elegant floral motifs. Here, in posy formation, tied with ribbons at the base, plate glasses are contained within two 'palm leaf' branches, with light-hearted curling acanthus-leafed cartouches and crestings.

Large looking-glasses were often made to go on piers above console tables between windows. These pier-glasses become windows in the evening when the curtains are shut, and with their tables below form an integral part of the room's decoration. Fig 103 shows a splendid Chippendale pier-glass, wonderfully charged with garden and chinoiserie motifs. While there are lesser birds below on stems of palm leaf with roses, and a naive little duck sits in a nest at the base, huge Chinese ho-ho birds flank the top with a central pagoda cresting.

A conventional yet charming combination of mirror-plate and marine

101 The carver's art has here created massive but light curling branches,
to hold candles to light a room for the Duke of Leeds at Hornby Castle.

102, 103, 104 Mirror plates, made by an expensive and dangerous
mercury process, were always highly valued and given special frames.
The Chippendale period variations here display a wealth of carved
giltwood ornament, ranging from elegant palm leaves and ribbon bows,
flowers and scrolls, to the elaborate fantasies of chinoiserie pagodas and
ho-ho birds.

painting is shown in fig 104. The glass is enclosed within rococo garlands of English garden flowers, decorating a more formal framework of carved flat-leafed designs. This landscape mirror was made to go above a fireplace, as was another (fig 105) which is much more fanciful. The latter is of a design associated with Thomas Johnson, who is famed for light rococo designs, often including winding tree and branch motifs. This splendid mirror combines such elements with chinoiserie rooflets over small balconies, and leafy scrollwork supporting a number of small brackets which were, no doubt, made to hold small oriental blue and white vases. In the centre is a larger niche flanked by steps and with gothic arcading above.

Chinoiserie giltwood was carried to extraordinary extremes, often with delightful, even elegant, whimsicality, and sometimes with a degree of ridiculous fun. In the best cases a sense of delight in the exotic and unknown fantasies of the East is the genuine basis for charming works of art. Icicles of carved giltwood are seen dripping from countless garden grottos.

Icicles are the common feature of two splendid pairs of torchères from Mallett's. Both are supported by scrolling cartouches but the first pair (fig 106), which came from Mentmore Towers, Buckinghamshire, consists of elegantly dressed Chinese figures holding up the lamp-stands; while the second (fig 107) is in the form of entwined fish, frozen into a secure balancing act. Both pairs of torchères fulfil their real purpose of holding up lights in an utterly charming decorative spirit, acting as silent servants.

Also decorative, but without a whisper of frivolity, is the very elegant pair

105 A splendid landscape or overmantel mirror, in the manner of Thomas Johnson, combines in carved giltwood Chinese pagodas and a gothic temple, flanked by realistic trees.

106-108 Rococo chinoiserie is epitomised by these delightful Chinese servants in the form of torcheres to support lights. Entwined dolphins fulfil the same purpose; and an elegant wall-bracket would have held a vase or perhaps a Chinese porcelain bird.

109 (opposite) Beds were among the most treasured possessions in a house, and no expense was spared on them, but ones of carved giltwood are seldom seen. This one, attributed to John Linnell, came from Keddleston Hall, Derbyshire.

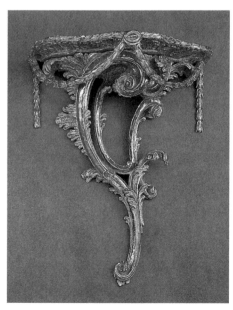

of wall-brackets (fig 108). Lightly carved, though adequately substantial, the wooden brackets are given an air of great delicacy. Leafy scrolls support flat shelves, hung with little swags of husks. The swags, of classical origin so much adopted by neo-classical architects and furniture designers alike, are derived from the botanical *garrya elliptica*. These brackets, circa 1760, were probably made to hold oriental porcelain vases or perhaps colourful Chinese birds. The transition from the rococo taste to the neo-classical, as advocated particularly by Robert Adam, but also by Thomas Chippendale in his later designs, was a fairly gradual process. Many pieces of furniture show elements of both fashions, and very often it is a combination of a certain stiffness and formality decorated both with scrolling motifs and with more restrained classical motifs which gives a particularly English sense of freedom.

The bed in fig 109 is circa 1770. It came from Kedleston Hall, Derbyshire and is attributed to John Linnell, following Robert Adam's re-modelling of the house for Lord Scarsdale. It has a splendid carved giltwood cresting, and the headboard and bed-end have equally fine mouldings of giltwood at the top and bottom. The posts of the bed are classical columns in white and gold, and the over-all mood of the design is distinctly transitional. The giltwood armchairs of fig 110 show a leaning towards neo-classicism, with square tapering legs but with shaped backs not entirely squared. In England the stricter lines adopted from Louis XVI fashions were somewhat softened, and the transition to neo-classicism was less sudden and rarely as severe.

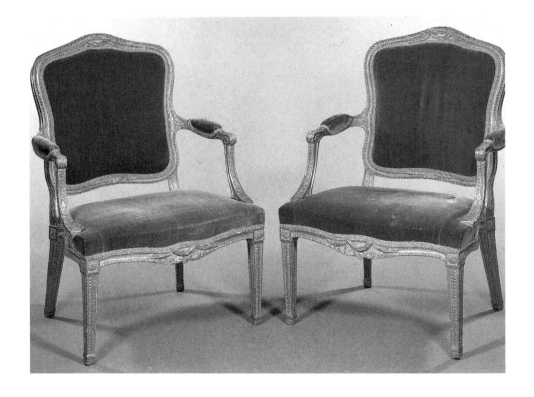

110 An elegant pair of transitional armchairs, displaying neo-classical motifs in a form reminiscent of an earlier fashion.

*111 A late 18th-century English armchair clearly inspired by French
models.*

In figs 111 and 112 the chair and sofa each have elements of neo-classicism combined with the flowing lines of earlier 18th-century designs. The armchairs (fig 110) are very richly carved with flutings around the seat frames, while the legs terminating in scroll feet and the shaped backs are also finely carved with mouldings and leaves.

The pair of torchères in fig 113 is representative of the full-bodied neo-classicism of Robert Adam and his contemporaries. Here English furniture is almost entirely an imitative reworking of what was considered a genuine classical form with elements derived from Greece and Rome. Rams' heads cap the tripod stands and classical urns are supported on joining stretchers, while the finer regular moulding patterns are of stylized leaves.

112 and 113 (opposite and above) An elegant sofa, with welcoming curved ends and flowing serpentine back, also incorporates the cool sophistication of neo-classical elements that were the hallmark of Robert Adam. These are even more distinctly displayed in the torchères opposite. The pair of armchairs, opposite, retain cabriole legs, shaped backs and curved arms, but are enriched with classical flutings and a honeysuckle motif on the legs.

THE AGE OF MAHOGANY

*T*he wood most highly prized for English furniture making in the 18th century was undoubtedly mahogany. Indeed this wood has been in continuous use ever since Indian imports were considerably increased in the 1720s. There are several varieties of the mahogany tree, but the best wood has many qualities particularly suited to the cabinet maker: it is closely grained and of the right strength for carving; it can be sawn in a way that displays fine figuring; and above all it can be polished to display a beautiful natural variation of tones. The colour itself can vary between rather dark brown almost black, Cuban wood of great density, to a relatively light open-grained texture suitable for certain flat surfaces. In sheet form in veneers, or in solid plank form as used in traditional 18th-century mahogany dining tables, a wonderful plane of wood figuration can be achieved. With judicious use of straight and curled grain, a long series of tops and leaves can be put together harmoniously and polished to create a spectacular work of art derived from natural resources, in a delightfully simple and lasting way (see fig 114). The hidden glories of the mahogany tree are revealed and displayed by man's ingenuity.

The use of mahogany is so closely associated with the designs and products of England's most famous furniture designer, Thomas Chippendale, that should you be overheard discussing antiques by the man on the Clapham

114 A long mahogany pedestal dining-table of about 1780 is here combined with a set of Chippendale period side-chairs. Originally the chairs would have been drawn up from the walls to a number of smaller tables.

omnibus, he would probably assume you were talking about mahogany furniture. However, the relatively small number of pieces discussed and illustrated here shows that mahogany only plays a part, albeit an important one, in the story of fine English furniture. Oak, walnut, giltwood lacquer, satinwood, painted and all sorts of other furniture share in the glories of furniture making. Nevertheless, it is certainly true that this imported wood, has a special status. Although highly prized and expensive, mahogany became fairly widely available, and some large items of furniture were made from it. Indeed fitments of interior decoration – libraries, doorcases, and even staircases – were made of mahogany, as well as smaller valued objects such as chairs and tables. In addition even precious boxes such as tea caddies were made of this prized wood.

William Vile and John Cobb made celebrated pieces of mahogany furniture for the royal family. Still in the royal collection today, these pieces display the full versatility both of Georgian cabinet making and of the wood itself. Fine carving on Queen Charlotte's cabinet, for example, and also on a magnificent bookcase made for George III, are seen in contrast to flat surfaces

115 Early mahogany furniture sometimes reflects architectural forms reminiscent of William Kent, as in this cabinet which has a writing compartment in the frieze.

veneered with finely figured and grained cross-bandings and mouldings. Plain surfaces are sometimes quartered to provide interesting contrasted figuration and colour.

A splendid cabinet which we had at Mallett's (fig 115) is representative of a relatively early use of mahogany. Somewhat reminiscent of William Kent, or perhaps of William Vile himself, the cabinet has palladian features, including a broken pediment flanked by scrolling consoles, heavy architectural swags and flowers, and, on the door fronts, finely figured oval panels framed within carved mouldings and spandrels. Small female masks and mouldings of Vitruvian scrolls and flutings were also popular in the 1740s. This period, the reign of George II, is characterised by features such as a combination of plain veneering and rich bold carving.

Fig 116, a side-table with a marble top, is also representative, having similar features together with bold cabriole legs, making the piece stand nobly and well. The crisp carving on the knee, the claw foot, and the flowing leaves in the apron give this side-table a delightful poise and dignity.

A delightful small Gainsborough armchair, upholstered with its original

116 This boldly shaped side-table displays the glories of crisp carving achievable in rich Cuban mahogany.

needlework, shows a restrained use of mahogany in an elegant form (fig 117). The chair has a certain amount of carved detail but none that could distract the eye from the fine needlework, which was possibly made by the wife of the patron who had the chair made.

Fig 118 shows contrasting uses of mahogany. The oval gate-leg table has a delightful simplicity and practicality which calls for nothing more than a display of the fine natural grains of the wood and its superb colour; while the mahogany sofa, which is part of a suite of hall furniture, is a splendid architectural item in neo-classical form. The finely carved legs in baluster form, perhaps reflecting the staircase that was nearby, and the exaggerated scrolls in the top of the seat rail, are deliberately contrasted with the magnificent figuring of the plain surfaces on the back of the piece. A leather cushion may have been placed on the seat of the sofa, as on many hall chairs, although there is no indentation in the seat to indicate this.

117 A magnificent garden of flowers, created in needlework, is incorporated in this elegant mahogany chair of about 1765.

118 (opposite) Wonderful figuration and colour are shown on a traditional oval gate-leg table; and also (below) in a more sophisticated neo-classical hall bench which is enriched with carved details.

A magnificent pair of Chippendale period mahogany serpentine chests of drawers or commodes (fig 119) are representative of the finest country house furniture. These chests, which were made for the Earl of Craven, display a wonderful use of mahogany. Again, plain surfaces of finely figured veneers and solid woods are contrasted with the carving on the canted front corners. These nobly proportioned chests are supported by large ogee bracket feet, and the clear-lacquered brass handles on the drawer fronts and on the brushing slides above add an extra degree of richness.

Further spectacular uses of veneering and carving are shown on an extremely fine Chippendale period mahogany card table (fig 120). Delicately shaped mouldings carved finely with a floral pattern, and acanthus leaves and carving on the elegant cabriole legs which taper to scrolling toes, all serve as a foil to the carefully selected pieces of curl veneer which are laid around the frieze of the table and on the upper surface. The back legs open in concertina action to support the folding top, which is lined on the inside with baize for playing games.

Curiously, another spectacular piece of Chippendale period furniture, a wardrobe (fig 121), is actually made of walnut, rather than mahogany. This splendid gentleman's clothes press is nonetheless closely related to a design in Chippendale's *The Gentleman and Cabinet-Maker's Director* of 1754, plate

119 and 120 (opposite) Traditional mahogany furniture is exemplified by one of a pair of chests of drawers of serpentine form, and a folding card table. These pieces show both fine carving and superb colour in the woodwork.

121 (above) An elaborate clothes press, related to a design by Thomas Chippendale, was curiously made in old-fashioned walnut, but to wonderful effect (circa 1760).

CXXXI. The bombé form of the base and the lively carved and applied mouldings on the door fronts are strongly reminiscent of the finest rococo carving. This press might easily have been made of mahogany but for some unknown reason the rather more old-fashioned walnut was chosen, and to great effect.

One of the great benefits of mahogany is that it is strong even when used in narrow gauge, such as table or chair legs. The next four illustrations show characteristic tables and a jardinière of the Chippendale period. Fig 122 is a splendid, large 'pie crust' table, so called because the moulding of the top resembles the edge of a pie. Supported by a fluted column, the stem rests on a tripod base, the cabriole legs of which terminate in claw and ball feet. A cartouche is carved on the knees and the top of the table displays good figuring and colour. The second tripod table (fig 123) provides an interesting variation, having a top resembling the shape of a tudor rose with a beaded

122 A Chippendale period tripod table, with a pie-crust top supported by a classical column.

moulding at the edge. Once again there is a column stem; this one has, at its base, a spiral turned urn shape supported by scrolling, inwardly turned legs. The mahogany wine cooler, jardinière, or possibly font, of fig 125, is an amazing *tour de force* of carving, having almost every feature of the carver's or silversmith's art applied to it. The crispness of the acanthus-leaf support to the bowl and all the other secondary motifs in the decoration is extraordinary, although, fortunately, restrained within the flowing lines of the basic design. Certainly this item must have been made at considerable expense for an appreciative patron who wanted something remarkable. Perhaps clues will one day lead to the identification of the designer or the origin of this special piece of furniture.

Fig 124 shows a fine quality mahogany dumb waiter with three graded revolving tiers suspended on a turned central column, each with a baluster gallery to prevent decanters or bottles from falling off.

123 (left) Another tripod table has a tudor rose-shaped top and inward curving scroll legs.

124 (right) A revolving three-tier dumb waiter, with spindle galleries around each shelf, circa 1770.

I have indicated that sometimes very substantial pieces were made of mahogany. Large break-front bookcases are not rare but of course they vary greatly in quality. An especially splendid example was handled by Mallett's recently. It is one of two similar designs of slightly different proportions and quality. Our piece (fig 126) is made of superb wood and has generous proportions. It is surmounted at the top by a huge carved urn in semi-relief and carved within a medallion in a humped pediment. Swags and husks along the top continue a neo-classical theme. The diamond-shaped fenestration of the glazed doors and the carved mouldings on the door fronts, and on the base, place this fine piece of furniture in the highest rank of mid-18th-century design and craftsmanship.

125 This unusual item, with an open bowl top, is elegantly drawn and as richly carved and chased as a precious gold object.

126 (opposite) A large break-front bookcase shows an extravagant use of fine wood in creating charming confidence and elegance for a practical purpose.

Also on a large scale, although requiring less precious mahogany, is a fine four-poster bed with carved mahogany front posts and an elaborately pierced, carved mahogany cresting of rococo form (fig 127). Bedroom furniture was made in great quantities and there are a number of mahogany chests, bedside cabinets, bed steps, torchères, chairs, and stools that were made specifically for use in bedrooms. Fig 128 shows a magnificent pair of mahogany torchères, crisply turned and carved. The tripod legs have extraordinary elegance with up-turned scrolled toes, and the legs are splayed sufficiently to support the tall stands which had to hold candles safely.

127 (opposite) A large four-poster bed is supported by carved mahogany columns, and bears an elaborate rococo cresting.

128 Simplicity of line is the essence of this pair of candle stands, but on close inspection there is a high degree of quality in the design and execution.

129 A deceptively carefree manipulation of design is a feature of this pair
of mahogany side chairs.

130 A pair of 'Gainsborough' library chairs from St Giles House, Dorset,
attributed to Thomas Chippendale.

Chair making is very much an art in itself, distinct from cabinet making; and the sculptural forms of chairs hold a great fascination for me. The varieties are enormous and the character that can be achieved in shaping chair backs and legs is unlimited. The chairs illustrated in fig 129 can be associated with the designs of Robert Manwaring. They are part of a set of four and are notable for the intertwining scrolling in their backs that almost seems to form monograms. The basic outline of the chair back is close to the traditional Queen Anne or George I shape, but the lively in-filling of the design, together with the Chippendale-type cabriole legs and the squared drop-in seats, show an interesting combination of elements.

Library armchairs, or 'Gainsborough chairs', can be very noble in proportion and large sets of these chairs were supplied in considerable numbers for bigger rooms. Figs 130 and 131 illustrate chairs associated with two famous houses, and it is known that relatively large sets were made of each design. The ones in fig 131, are attributed to John Gordon, who made similar chairs for the Duke of Atholl, which are still at Blair Castle, Perthshire, and are upholstered with needlework that was worked by the then Duchess. The frames of all these chairs are carved with a scale pattern neatly following the serpentine lines of the seat frames and the graceful legs. The armchairs illustrated have been upholstered with contemporary Soho tapestry.

131 Chairs with scale pattern carving of this design were supplied to the Duke of Atholl, to display needlework made by his wife.

The two chairs in fig 130 are from a famous set made for St Giles, in Dorset, and are attributed to Thomas Chippendale. They are magnificently carved with flowers, shells, and fronds along the seat rails, and with swags of flowers and a trellis design on the legs and on the arms.

Fig 132 shows a graceful mid-18th-century Chippendale period armchair with an elegant, carved, shaped frieze and very finely carved legs. The pair of chairs in fig 134 is considerably plainer, although representative of many fine Chippendale chairs. The straight, square legs and upward curving arms are carefully moulded, which is both practical and attractive, with a surface which catches light in an interesting way. These chairs are especially notable for their interesting 18th-century needlework coverings, depicting agricultural scenes within roundels framed by flower designs.

Earlier I referred to a magnificent Chippendale period cabinet in the Chinese style (page 34). This remarkable piece of furniture (fig 133) is the epitome of chinoiserie taste, incorporating many elements of Chinese fantasy. It is made of padouk (or possibly sabicu), resembling mahogany in colour but even richer in textural variety. Conceived in the Chinese manner in pagoda form, it has elaborate carved giltwood chinoiserie rooves, fenestration, and decoration on the base, some of it incorporating gothic motifs. A central

132 A mid 18th-century armchair, where the wood is elegantly carved like upholstery fringing around the seat.

133 (opposite) A tour de force of chinoiserie is presented in this splendid cabinet of padouk, with giltwood pagodas and mouldings, from Kenure Park in Ireland.

drawer, beneath the display shelves enclosed by the glazed doors, contains a writing slide. The cabinet stands on most unusual cluster legs with gilt frond bindings, terminating in feet consisting of rocks and pebbles. The inspiration for the cabinet must be related to plate CXXXV of Chippendale's *Director* (1754). It is 9ft 8in high, and formerly stood at Kenure Park, Rush, Co Dublin.

Similar pagoda-like trellis is incorporated in the backs of Chippendale chairs. Fig 135 shows a single side-chair, no doubt originally one of an extended set. This chair has a back in the form of a Chinese pavilion made up of a pagoda roof, arches and a trellis fence at the base. The legs are formed of a fanciful group of cluster columns. The armchairs of fig 136 have Chinese trellis – or *treillage* – backs giving an exotic air of whimsy to an otherwise fairly conventional form. The square tapering legs seen here were to become a standard feature of later 18th-century chairs.

As we have seen, it was a happy characteristic of the Georgian era that almost everything created in that period, be it architecture or artefact, writing, music, or other work of art, was made in a graceful manner with a natural elegance and eloquence. There is, as a result, great charm and quality even in relatively ordinary things, which were usually made with good proportions and a certain beauty of line.

134 Well-proportioned but relatively simple mahogany chair frames are here upholstered with interesting original needlework.

135 and 136 The term Chinese Chippendale is admirably exemplified by these chairs of the 1760s. In both cases, the adaptation of Chinese motifs is elegantly contained within a traditional format.

Two representative clocks, a grandfather and a bracket clock, both in mahogany cases, have a restraint and elegance due to the use of fine materials beautifully worked. In each example the clock has delightful proportions. The longcase clock (fig 137) has a tall slim case and the hood is crowned with a chinoiserie and pretty pierced fretwork pagoda cresting. The bracket clock in fig 139 has a handsome simplicity, a fine movement, and charming brass bracket feet.

A great number of handsome pedestal desks and writing tables were made in relatively plain and conventional forms. They are usually rectangular with a central kneehole, and have cupboards for folios on one side and a series of drawers on the other. Some desks are large enough for two people to work at, one each side; these are referred to as partners' desks. An outstanding large-scale writing desk or library table is shown in fig 138. This especially fine example of classic mahogany furniture is attributed to Thomas Chippendale himself, and is closely related to plate LXXXIII in *The Gentleman and Cabinet-Maker's Director*, 1754. It was made for the fifth Baron Craven of Combe Abbey (1705-1769), and formed part of a group of mid-18th-century furniture supplied to him after designs in Chippendale's *Director*. The desk is 8ft long with concave canted corners, and the two pedestals each contain three cupboards faced with carved flower and leaf ovals flanked by corbels. The cupboards enclose drawers and shelves.

Round drum tables on tripod legs, or rent tables sometimes on square box plinths, were frequently found in entrance halls or in libraries and reading rooms. Fig 140 shows an octagonal rent table, the drawers indexed with letters engraved on ivory labels to be used for filing tenants' papers. In the centre of the leather top there is a central well for keeping cash received from rents.

More unusual items of furniture include musical instruments. Relatively few have survived, since they were superseded by later improved versions. The delightful 18th-century spinet made by Baker Harris of London dated 1766 (fig 141) is given an elegant mahogany case with a lift-up top in order to let out more sound if required, and the instrument rests on a separate stand, also of mahogany, with cabriole legs carved on the knees and at the feet. Another Baker Harris instrument, dated 1770, is in the Victoria and Albert Museum.

The elegant flowing lines of Louis XV furniture had considerable influence on English furniture making. In contrast to the straight forms of the splendid chests illustrated in fig 119, we see an alternative, slightly later variety, much more delicate in design (fig 142). 'In the French taste', this largish chest of drawers is made light and graceful by a serpentine front, shaped sides, and

137 A pagoda cresting is part of the restrained ornament of a mahogany longcase clock of about 1765.

138 The magnificent desk or library table from Combe Abbey is closely related to a design by Thomas Chippendale, 1754.

139 A mahogany bracket clock.

140 The top of this octagonal rent table revolves for easy access to the lettered drawers, and in the centre there is a well for cash collected by the landlord.

gently curving front legs. A shaped apron around the bottom frieze also adds
grace. The three commodious long drawers are veneered with consecutive
pages of fine veneer, giving the effect over the three drawers of a massive
fountain of light. The top is similarly veneered with finely figured mahogany.
Above the drawers is a long brushing slide, both practical and elegant.

The two pairs of chairs illustrated in fig 143 and 144 both have delicacy
and charm. The first pair is in curvilinear form in the French taste with
wonderfully shaped mahogany frames displaying only a thin banding of

*141 Musical instruments such as this spinet by Baker Harris are among
many practical items that must have disappeared as their usefulness
became outdated.*

wood around the edge of the upholstery, which is very finely carved with gadroon moulding. The legs and arm supports, the most visible parts of the chair, are elegantly curved with flowing lines. The shield-back armchairs of fig 144 also stand extremely gracefully, and the woodwork, though constructed robustly, is made to look delicate and almost insubstantial. The craftsmanship is of the highest level, achieving a graceful appearance without losing strength. These chairs stand on pointed tapering legs dancing just as lightly as their rococo predecessors in the previous illustration.

142 A useful chest of drawers becomes a work of art when given curvilinear lines and veneered with best quality mahogany. Circa 1770.

143 and 144 Being a strong wood, mahogany suited the chair-maker admirably. He could ingeniously create a light curved design of great complexity, and also maintain considerable strength. The lightness of these shield-back chairs and upholstered armchairs, with gadrooned carving (fig 144), is remarkable. Both models were made in extensive sets.

A further pair of chairs (fig 145), probably originally part of a set, are of comparable form, but demonstrate the wide variations that were made in shape and detail. The shield or escutcheon backs are in this case filled with boldly carved Prince of Wales feathers, the three plumes gathered within a coronet. Although unusually prominent and extremely decorative this badge does not necessarily refer to royal ownership, as it was generally adopted by furniture makers of the late 18th century for ornamental purposes in carving and inlay.

Of the same period but made for more informal use, and of a less decorative nature, are tub chairs. Fig 146 shows a fine example. The back and seat are entirely upholstered over a beechwood frame, but the exposed seat rail, the legs and the arm supports are of mahogany. All the visible wood is superbly carved with fine details including flutings on round tapering legs of Louis XVI type. The arm supports are also carved in neo-classical manner with an interesting rope motif of Greek origin.

The name Thomas Chippendale is closely associated with the flamboyant, happy decoration of the rococo period – dancing scrolls, flowers, posies, ribbons, chinoiserie, and gothic fantasies. These elements seem the hallmark of Chippendale furniture, though we should also remember plainer and more sober pieces with straight lines. Despite the popular rococo image of Thomas Chippendale, he was, in fact, a supplier of much furniture in the neo-classical taste, and most of his documented pieces, including furniture made for

145 A pair of mahogany armchairs boldly emblazoned with the Prince of Wales feathers, a popular motif of the last quarter of the 18th century.

128

Harewood House in Yorkshire, are in this style. This later, plainer style and decoration was largely derived from classical origins in Italy, where patrons and architectural students had been studying the new finds of Herculaneum, Pompeii, and others while making the grand tour. Travellers collected classical sculpture and fragments of architecture assiduously, then attempted to recreate classical decoration within their Georgian houses in a most novel and exciting way. This neo-classicism was at the core of the Louis XVI period in France. In England its most famous advocate was the Scottish architect, Robert Adam. To an even greater extent than Chippendale, Adam had tremendous influence, not only on architecture but on every facet of the decorative arts. Though there was still occasion for the use of the rococo in decoration, the neo-classical trend was dominant in the last three decades of the 18th century.

146 A mahogany tub chair derived in form from the French bergère. The framework is of beech, with mahogany used for the parts that show.

Neo-Classicism and the Sheraton Period

*B*eing an island, England always had a distinct independence and idiosyncrasy in its decorative arts. With this was combined a certain domesticity which resulted in a national style that was peculiarly individual. It was free of the many conventions adopted in Europe, and was, above all, rather more naturally expressive. Unlike in France, the development of the decorative arts was not bound by strict convention. Cabinet makers were not restricted by strongly enforced guild rules, nor did designers feel bound to follow the conventional requirements of court circles. French furniture certainly rose to heights of unparalleled excellence in the 18th century, and superb pieces, true works of art, were made. Much of this, however, was so grand that it bears little relevance outside palatial settings, and it needs to be viewed within the context of its complementary architecture, boiseries, and room interiors. Though the same can be true of English furniture, fortunately it is in general much more adaptable and 'accessible'. As a result it can be appreciated in almost every conceivable setting, historical or modern.

In many ways English furniture is softer and gentler in appearance, has more charm, and is easier to live with. French furniture has, however, had a great influence on English furniture, and at times there were considerable interchanges of design elements and taste. Mallett's has sold a certain amount

147 The golden tones of satinwood imported from the West Indies are well displayed in this bookcase of about 1780. Mahogany is used in the framework and provides some of the darker detailing.

of French furniture over the years, especially fine provincial furniture but also some more elaborate pieces. We have not, however, specialised in the most important works of the French *ébénistes* (cabinet makers), and have not sold many pieces with the provenance of Versailles or from the great chateaux.

However, in 1971, the Art Institute of Chicago did acquire from us a magnificent royal commode signed by Jean-Henri Riesener, 1734-1806, made master *ébéniste* in 1768. This superb piece of furniture (fig 148) contains two large drawers and three smaller drawers in the frieze, and is surmounted by a white marble top; the sides and drawer fronts are inlaid with floral marquetry; the ormolu mounts are of superb quality and include an elaborate frieze with paterae, caryatids at the canted corners, and lions' paw feet on the

148 A magnificent French commode by Jean-Henri Riesener was an unusual treasure at Mallett's that is now to be seen at the Art Institute of Chicago.

legs; a winged mask is suspended on the lower frieze. The marquetry is of the richest quality and contains a great variety of woods.

We have had many remarkable pieces of English furniture closely allied to French furniture and inspired by French cabinet making. The commode shown in fig 149 is in an English transitional style, being essentially of Louis XVI form, that is, with straight sides and having a rectangular appearance rather than being shaped, but it has cabriole legs. Another notable feature of this chest, which would not have been true of its French counterpart, is that the top is of wood rather than marble, inlaid with marquetry. The commode is of mahogany, satinwood, and harewood (dyed sycamore), and is inlaid on all sides with posies and vases of flowers. It is further enriched with ormolu

149 An English commode that clearly derives many of its features from French furniture, including formal marquetry panels and the use of gilt bronze, or ormolu, mounts. Circa 1770.

mounts in the French manner, but less opulently, and more in keeping with English taste.

Pierre Langlois was a French cabinet maker who came to London because of the French Revolution, and formed a business in St Martin's Lane where several English cabinet makers had workshops. Here he quickly found patrons who desired the high quality furniture influenced by his French background, both in form and decoration. Langlois was famous in English country houses for supplying splendid commodes and lesser items which had something of the appearance of French furniture, but, invariably, had wooden – not marble – tops, lighter ormolu fittings and a restraint not used on furniture made in France.

Many of his commodes are of serpentine shape and have bombé sides. Fig 150 shows one of a pair of small commodes of this kind. It is restrained but exceedingly elegant, with delicate scrolls of marquetry in the doors and on the top. The simple, gentle lines are not cluttered by ormolu mounts on the corners; only a plain beaded brass moulding divides and protects the crossbanding between the two doors on the front. Pierre Langlois was perhaps the maker of a set of four magnificent commodes which were acquired by George IV for Buckingham Palace. These wonderfully exuberant pieces have emphasised scrolls at the sides; one is dated 1763. A similar magnificent commode, obviously made in the same workshop around the same time, was at Mallett's some years ago (fig 151). It is of serpentine form veneered in rosewood, with a fleur de pêche marble top mounted with an ormolu border of an egg and dart moulding. All four corners consist of huge double scrolls

150 A pair of bombé commodes, in the 'French taste', decorated with marquetry. English, circa 1770.

outlined with ormolu acanthus leaves, mouldings and paterae. The doors and sides of the piece are decorated with centred ormolu foliate roundels flanked by stylized leaf sprays. The apron below the doors is mounted with an ormolu mask and foliate scrolls.

Several other less important but nonetheless fine pieces of furniture are associated with Pierre Langlois. Fig 152 shows a small occasional table containing a writing drawer in the top. Similar in line to a Louis XV occasional table, this charming piece reflects French taste closely yet has a certain restraint that makes it unquestionably English. The top is kingwood inlaid with marquetry and the gentle cabriole legs terminate in modest sabots with ormolu toes. Another occasional table, fig 153, is distinctly English in form though it clearly shows the French taste in its flowing lines. Variations of this kind of table were made for many years, sometimes with workbags hanging from a drawer, and on other occasions with screens fitted which

151 An extraordinary rosewood commode with elaborate mounts, one of a related group, and similar to four at Buckingham Palace which are attributed to Pierre Langlois. Circa 1765.

could be pulled up to protect the user from the heat of the fire. In this case, the table is fitted with a drawer and a slide in one side, while on the other two sides there are dummy mouldings and handles. The back is plain.

A great deal of English furniture reflected the French taste, and 18th-century furniture designers in their pattern books regularly offered drawings 'in the French manner' or 'in the French taste'. Large suites of furniture were made with the curvilinear lines derived from Louis XV chairs, yet with a certain openness in scale and lacking what I sometimes feel is a French doll-like quality. That to me makes the English designs especially pleasing.

A very fine set of six giltwood armchairs, together with a pair of large giltwood sofas, from Harewood House, Yorkshire, have passed through Mallett's hands on two occasions. This suite, which was perhaps designed by Thomas Chippendale around 1770, is upholstered with fine floral needlework probably circa 1800-1820, although it is possible that it is earlier. The six chairs (fig 154), combine an elegant design with fine, though restrained, carving in the giltwood, and with their needlework coverings must have made a most handsome impression in a room where they were undoubtedly only part of the overall scheme.

152 and 153 Two occasional tables of Louis XV shape and proportions, but distinctly English in workmanship.

154 (opposite) Two giltwood armchairs, part of a suite of furniture from Harewood House, Yorkshire where Chippendale provided much furniture, upholstered with floral needlework in tones of green and pink on a white background.

Of the same period, though very different in feeling, is a splendid pair of mahogany shield-back armchairs, boldly carved with Prince of Wales feathers filling the backs which I referred to on page 128 and illustrated (fig 145). The somewhat cooler design of these beautiful chairs has a clear cut elegance in the shield back, the light arms, and the delicate pointed square tapering legs. All of these features can be associated with the designer George Hepplewhite (died 1786) whose pattern book, *Cabinet Maker and Upholsterers' Guide* had considerable influence and is looked upon as a landmark in furniture history.

Hepplewhite was a keen advocate of the flowing shapes of mid-18th-century furniture but also promoted the straight lines suggested by the neo-classicism of subsequent years, simplified and made feminine and elegant in an especially Georgian manner. This feeling was taken up even more strongly by Thomas Sheraton (1751-1806), who is associated with the use of light-coloured woods, particularly satinwood in delicate, airy designs. His work is synonymous with Georgian elegance in English furniture. Sheraton satinwood furniture preceded by Chippendale mahogany furniture must be considered the pinnacle of English cabinet and chair making.

Perhaps the most significant piece of satinwood furniture which we have had, and certainly the most historic, is the original Carlton House writing table, fig 155. Mallett's acquired the desk from the descendants of Admiral

155 The Carlton House desk which was given to Admiral Payne by the Prince Regent, later George IV. This form of writing table henceforth derived its name from the Prince's residence, Carlton House. The handles on this piece are of silver.

*156 A magnificent cabinet of half-round form, with a
writing section, very elaborately inlaid with neo-classical
designs in a wide variety of woods (circa 1780).*

Payne. It is said to have been made for George IV in the 1790s when he was Prince of Wales and was living at Carlton House. Documentation regarding the provenance of the desk has not been found, but it is known that the Prince Regent gave it to Admiral Payne for his service in accompanying the Prince's future wife, Princess Caroline of Brunswick, to England from her home.

This large and important piece of furniture is splendidly proportioned and is presumably the prototype of the many variations of Carlton House desk made subsequently. The lining is mahogany and the veneering satinwood, and it is decorated only with fine cross-bandings and elegant silver handles on the drawer fronts. These are hallmarked with the maker's initials and all bear the Prince's coronet. It is very likely that the desk was made to a design by Thomas Sheraton.

Another outstanding piece of satinwood furniture (fig 156) is a remarkable cabinet which is one of three known, the other two being at the Metropolitan Museum, New York, and at Luton Hoo, Bedfordshire. These cabinets, together with a few other pieces of furniture with related designs, must have been made by an important cabinet maker who is yet to be identified. The piece illustrated is in the form of a half-round commode with a superstructure containing a cupboard, numerous drawers and a shelf above. The whole piece is superbly inlaid with very fine marquetry in an unusual variety of woods. The motifs shown in the marquetry show a broad understanding of neo-classical subjects and include classical urns, swags of *garrya elliptica,* Corinthian pilasters, and vines. The upper part of the commode section contains a pull-out writing drawer which is enclosed behind sliding tambour doors. The elaborate hidden locking devices and the good gilt brass mounts are interesting. A bust of Bacchus, adorned with grapes, surmounts the entire piece as a finial at the top.

As well as marquetry, painted furniture also provided colourful decoration. My next chapter will concentrate specifically on that. Here marquetry and painted work combine in a splendid four-poster bed (fig 158). The satinwood front posts are inlaid with floral marquetry, and the bed has a magnificent carved and painted cresting in an undulating serpentine form of the much-loved anthemion or honeysuckle motif. This charming pattern was the most universal decorative emblem of Robert Adam and neo-classicism. It is to be seen over and over again, worked into borders of plasterwork, furniture, textiles, and indeed every form of decoration. The motif was even used extensively in metalwork: in fire grates, in the brass fittings for doors, and on the iron railings outside houses. Relatively trivial pieces of furniture were given attention more appropriate for important pieces. Even fire screens (fig 157) were elegantly made with finely carved giltwood tripod bases, polished

157 A late 18th-century painted and gilt fire screen.

158 *A four-poster bed in the manner of Robert Adam, with satinwood front posts inlaid with marquetry, and a carved and painted cresting featuring the ubiquitous honeysuckle flower motif.*

159 and 160 Two late 18th-century 'demi-lune' commodes in neo-classical form. Fig 159 (above) is one of a pair having urns boldly inlaid on the fronts; while fig 160 (below) is of a large scale, with painted roundels adding focus to the mellow glow of the satinwood veneers.

brass poles supporting adjustable shields, charmingly painted in this case with a gentle bird, sprigs of leaves, and leafy borders.

Of about the same date, that is circa 1780, is a magnificent breakfront bookcase of mahogany and satinwood, finely inlaid with urns in the doors and base, and having prominent Vitruvian scrolling around the waist. At the top is a fan motif in an arch above swags and husks and marquetry flutings (fig 147). The bookcase is fitted in the lower part with a fall-front secretaire drawer, and the drawer-fronts have characteristic Sheraton period circular repoussé brass ring handles. These are decorated with urns, a very characteristic emblem of neo-classicism.

That same motif is the central subject in the decoration of a splendid half-round commode (fig 159). Delicately hanging by a ribbon from a small rope, it has a colossal medallion on the front containing a neo-classical urn. The top is similarly decorated with an architectural fan. The attractive wavy apron at the base of the piece is raised from the ground by modest turned tapering legs.

Fig 160 shows a particularly fine, large, half-round commode of satinwood which has a direct association with Thomas Chippendale. It is thought to have been supplied by him to Newby Hall, Yorkshire. On this piece there is little marquetry. Instead, contrasting veneers of satinwood of a wonderful colour and figuration are quartered on the door-fronts, and, in the centre of each, is a painted roundel showing mythological female figures painted in the manner of Angelica Kauffmann, who was famed for such work in association with Robert Adam.

However, most furniture was smaller and many useful domestic pieces of outstanding quality were made. We may take for example a series of tables: pembroke tables, centre tables, sofa tables, card tables, many kinds of occasional table, and an almost unlimited variety of others. The antique dealer or visitor to country houses is perpetually surprised at how he can often see something that had never before occurred to him and of which he had never dreamed. This is due to the imagination of patrons who made diverse demands on the ever-versatile designers and craftsmen of the 18th century.

Thomas Sheraton was a northerner from County Durham, but he moved to London around 1790 and lived at No 41 Davies Street, a little down the road from the present Mallett at Bourdon House. His very influential *Cabinet Maker and Upholster's Drawing Book* was published in parts between 1791 and 1794. In this work he presented an excellent selection of currently fashionable ideas, together with recommendations and suggestions. Many of the engravings show light elegant designs, often with straight tapering legs.

Among such are pembroke tables, so-called, according to Sheraton, after the Countess of Pembroke who 'first gave orders for one'. These smallish tables, which come in a variety of shapes, but always have flaps on either side to extend them, are especially useful occasional and adaptable pieces. At Mallett's we have had many fine examples and just a few may be cited.

Fig 161 shows a pembroke table with 'butterfly' shaped flaps. The satinwood top is inlaid with fine marquetry including a large patera in the centre roundel and urns within ovals on the flaps.

The frame of the table and the legs are generally of the same wood as the top though sometimes less richly inlaid or decorated. Another table, however (fig 162), with an oval top, has a giltwood base with fluted tapering columns for legs, carved at top and bottom with acanthus leaves. The lovely top is finely inlaid with marquetry and shows in the centre a splendid shell surrounded by swags of flowers and, overlapping the flap, classical fronds with urns. Around the edge of the table is an elaborate multiple cross-banding with delicate intertwining tendrils of flowers inlaid into the broadest band.

161 A charming shaped pembroke table of satinwood, with fine marquetry and cross-bandings. Circa 1780.

Sometimes groups or suites of furniture were made for a room. Pairs of side tables are frequently seen, also pairs of sofa tables and occasionally of card tables. Pairs of pembroke tables are rarer but we were once lucky enough to have a superb pair together with a card table en suite. These three pieces are of harewood (sycamore) superbly inlaid with neo-classical marquetry (fig 163). The three tables have a uniform design with central fan roundels, swags of husks, and rosettes in the borders.

A variation of the pembroke table is the so called spider-leg, gate-leg table. Fig 164 shows a fine satinwood example with the characteristic thin, hinged legs. The top of this piece is inlaid with bow and arrows harmlessly strewn with flowers.

Sofa tables were longer and, although made to be placed behind sofas, they were used for a variety of purposes. They were extremely adaptable and frequently treated as writing tables; some had interiors fitted with games compartments, a backgammon board lining the well and on the underside of the sliding top a squared board for playing chess or draughts. Fig 165 shows

162 An oval pembroke table that has the unusual combination of a giltwood base and wooden top decorated with marquetry.

145

one of rosewood with satinwood cross-banding and with a turned stretcher joining the two splay legs.

Drum and rent tables continued to be popular; a small satinwood example (fig 166) with a leather top stands on a slender pillar base with four claw legs terminating in brass toes and castors. Though furniture was much more abundantly made by the end of the 18th century, many pieces were still specially commissioned. An unusual satinwood table which came from Althop, Northamptonshire (fig 167), has a ratcheted fold-up top to support a drawing or heavy volume. Drawer fronts on one of the long sides are richly decorated with large brass swag handles, and the four square tapering legs end at the feet in particularly emphatic brass toes and large castors for easy running.

163 The top of this table, one of three, is extremely delicately inlaid with contrasting woods made pliable like silken embroidery.

A truly magnificent breakfast table (fig 168) is round with a most elegant single pillar support on four splay legs with brass toes and castors. The circular top has a plain satinwood centre with a broad cross-banding and a chased brass rim. The stem and legs are also cross-banded and lined in contrasting woods. As with many tables of this kind, the top is hinged and a lever on the underside allows it to be tilted upright for easier moving or storage. Fig 169 shows a smaller item, probably originally part of a set of dining room furniture. This is a pair of satinwood knife boxes in the form of urns. The tops lift up on central ratchet stems to reveal storage for cutlery. These knife boxes were probably placed on a sideboard or on flanking stands either side of the sideboard. The satinwood is especially finely figured and is delicately inlaid with lines of boxwood and ebony.

164 The feminine lightness of this folding spider-leg table is augmented by cupid's bow and two arrows inlaid into the satinwood top.

165-168 *There is no limit to the variety of late Georgian tables. Here we see a rosewood sofa table fitted with games, a small satinwood drum table, an unusual reading table with an adjustable folding top, and a splendid large round breakfast table on a single pedestal with four splayed legs.*

169 Elegantly formed satinwood urns, which open to hold cutlery.

170 The design for this side-table, one of a pair, is to be found in Sheraton's Drawing Book. The top is of rosewood with painted cross-banding, while the legs are gilded (circa 1800).

A pair of sidetables (fig 170) closely related to a design in Sheraton's *Drawing Book*, have rosewood tops with gilded legs and stretchers beneath. The tables are further enriched with bands of satinwood, overpainted with garlands of flowers. Painting on wood was an especially pretty and softening form of decoration. It was much imitated in Edwardian times but genuine 18th-century paintwork tends to have a greater elegance and simplicity, as seen on the satinwood pembroke table with canted corners in fig 171. Similarly there is fine painted decoration on a magnificent satinwood secretaire cabinet (fig 172). This has a book case in the top section, while in the lower part there is a secretaire drawer with a fall-front, and below that, cupboards.

An even more elaborate cabinet of this kind (fig 173) is one associated with Thomas Weekes who was famed for his museum. He is also remembered for a type of cabinet, of a certain shape and usually surmounted by a convex mirror or clock in the same manner as his building. These cabinets would have a bookcase above, secretaire drawer below, and, in some examples an organ fitted into the bottom cupboard. In this case there is no organ, which is probably fortunate since an organ would make the drawers above rather high. The quality of the woodwork is outstanding with a great variety of cross-banding and line inlay carried out even on the glazing bars of the windows.

171 The honey colour of a pembroke table is further enriched with painted floral decoration. Circa 1790.

172 Sheraton furniture is noted for its clear lines. This secretaire cabinet is of beautifully figured satinwood, with painted decoration.

173 (opposite) is a more elaborate piece made by Thomas Weekes, with complex cross-bandings, line decoration and a convex mirror at the top – a feature characteristic of the maker.

174 *A handsome pair of small satinwood commodes, redolent of Georgian elegance and hung with swags of husks attached by bows in marquetry.*

175 *(below) is a practical but highly decorative pair of small bookcases in satinwood, with graded shelving (circa 1780).*

A pair of small satinwood commodes (fig 174), and a pair of charming, small bookcases with graded shelves and cupboards and drawers below (fig 175), are excellent examples of fine domestic furniture not on the grand scale. Both are superb quality with the finest satinwood veneers, and, in the case of the commodes, elegant, Georgian marquetry typical of the Adam and Sheraton period with garlands of flowers and paterae. Polished brass handles further enliven the golden tones of the wood.

Before finishing this chapter I must include a most unusual pair of small cabinets profusely and intensely decorated in the classical manner with superb inlay (fig 176). These relatively small objects (about 2ft high) display a *tour de force* of marquetry with sphinxes, ewers, and other motifs inlaid in ivory amongst various woods on a mahogany base. The drawing of the decoration is of jewel-like precision. The cabinets stand on short turned legs below giltwood inverted consoles of acanthus.

176 One of a remarkable pair of small cabinets, inlaid with jewel-like precision with ivory and various textured woods, in high neo-classical fashion.

155

PAINTED FURNITURE

*P*olished wood cabinets, tables and chairs are naturally pre-eminent in furniture-making, and carved giltwood furniture suits the grander formality of many more architectural settings. Lacquer furniture also, as we have seen, played a prominent part from the 17th century. A further alternative, painted furniture, has, over the years, assumed an especially important position in the decorative arts. In some ways it is the most subtle and sophisticated of all furniture and can be used to create a wide variety of moods. Above all it played an important role in contributing to the design of rooms where a special atmosphere was wanted.

It could be elegant and decorative, yet not quite as formal as the chief saloons where giltwood and polished furniture were displayed. Painted furniture might be said to be less important, less substantial; but nonetheless particular artistry was called for in the achievement of decorative schemes which often had a lightness and cheerful warmth deliberately contrasting with more sober atmospheres achieved in neighbouring rooms. Indeed many great houses contained an enfilade of fine rooms which specifically accommodated furniture of different kinds. At Osterley Park, Middlesex, for instance, Robert Adam in his carefully conceived interiors provided rooms in sequence: one with superb mahogany, satinwood, and marquetry furniture, another with painted furniture in the Etruscan style, a state bedroom with

177 Painted furniture of semi-architectural form is often associated with William Kent, an architect whose creativity and influence carried into many fields from furniture to gardening. The woodwork of this table is painted and gilt, presumably consistent with the decoration of the room for which it and the companion table were conceived.

entirely gilded furniture, and elsewhere in the house much furniture was either in gilt and white painted or entirely painted. In each case the furniture was made to relate closely to the overall decoration of the room. With painted furniture it is particularly important to remember that the painted woodwork, and also the upholstery coverings, of course, were intended to continue and be an extension of the wall decoration, painted ceiling, and carpet.

More than any other furniture, painted furniture was designed to fit into schemes of interior decoration. A pair of console tables, for example, in the manner of William Kent (fig 177), is decorated in white and gold, the bold scrolling design with a shell in the centre and with a key pattern and rosette frieze supporting a marble top. They were certainly made to be placed against a specific wall in a room which was undoubtedly decorated, probably with panelling, dado rails and other mouldings, all in the same idiom. In some ways it is difficult to imagine these tables out of their designed setting, but adaptation is possible. Although the original setting may be lost, furniture can be placed again in alternative surroundings which create a new artistic ensemble.

Some painted furniture perpetuates the characteristics of lacquerwork in feeling. A painted clock, for example (fig 178), in a magnificent case with elaborate cut glass and gilt brass mounts, was made for the Turkish market.

178 An exotic painted bracket clock, with a cut-glass dome and finials, made for the Turkish market and with arabic numerals, by Markwick Markham.

*179 A leather screen decorated with an incongruous collection of birds
and animals in a flowery jungle.*

180 and 181 The vogue for chinoiserie furniture in the mid 18th century
is here represented by chairs made for Badminton House,
Gloucestershire, with japanned decoration; and by another pair (fig 181)
of curvilinear form with white decoration.

The movement is by Markwick Markham, circa 1740. Markham appears to have made many clocks for the Turkish market, and in this example the exotic glass finials are topped with crescent shaped moons while the clockface itself has Arabic numerals. The wooden case of the clock is decorated delicately with white flowers on a blue ground, and the face has painted decoration on a pink ground around the enamel dials. Another piece of painted furniture which could be said to be a descendant from oriental lacquer furniture is this unusual sixfold leather screen (fig 179). Possibly Spanish but more likely English, it is richly decorated on a gilded ground with monkeys and birds swinging on brightly flowering trees. The screen dates from the early part of the 18th century.

Much other painted furniture, while not strictly of japanned decoration, that is, not imitating lacquer, reflects elements of chinoiserie. Three outstanding pairs of Chippendale period armchairs are delightful examples. The first pair (fig 180) is from a famous suite of furniture made for the state bedroom apartment of Charles Somerset, 4th Duke of Beaufort, at Badminton House, Gloucestershire. The room was decorated in the exotic 'Chinese' manner of the early 1750s. Their Chinese-fret backs with pagoda crests were placed around the walls, which were hung with colourful Chinese paper decorated with flowers and birds. The splendid bed from the same room is now in the Victoria and Albert Museum. The suite of eight armchairs is thought to have originally been decorated in red. The black decoration is japanned with raised gilt chinoiseries. The raised motifs are built up with layers of gesso under gold leaf and painted decoration.

Fig 181 shows a variation of trellis, in this case adapted to European rococo fantasies, while the cabriole legs make little concession to this form but provide a well proportioned framework for the overall design. These chairs are entirely decorated with soft white paint nicely toned with aged. The third pair of chairs in this group (fig 182), all of which date from around 1760, shows yet further fantasies of chinoiserie trellis. The pierced backs and sides are echoed in blind fret carving around the seat frame and down the legs. Again these chairs are painted white but all the trellis-work is overlaid with gold leaf in contrast to the background colour.

Much Louis XV furniture was painted and each piece was made to fit within a surrounding of boiserie and fabrics. There is an elegant, dancing lightness in the armchairs or *fauteuils* illustrated in fig 183, which are probably English in fact though they could almost as easily have been French. On the whole, English chairs are slightly larger in scale and slightly less accentuated in form. In other respects, certainly as far as painting is concerned, there is little difference between England and France. These chairs

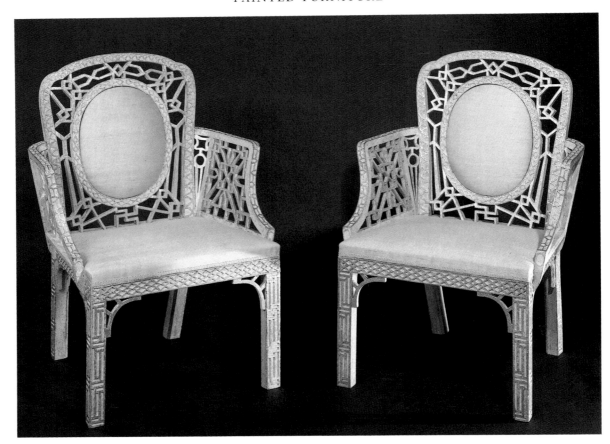

have frames painted in off-white or stone colour while the mouldings and carved decoration are of blue, now worn to an attractive greyish tone.

Fig 185 shows a pair of English bergère armchairs which, in the French taste, shows elements of both French and English forms. Of the Adam period, these chairs are essentially neo-classical, with fluted tapering legs and with neo-classical paterae and husks, but the shape of the backs is derived from earlier prototypes. The decoration in this case is red and white. The chairs came from Moccas Court, Herefordshire.

In England, extreme fantasies of 'Indian' chinoiserie taste reached a climax in the creation of the Prince Regent's Royal Pavilion at Brighton in the early 19th century. Anticipating this triumphant masterpiece, and undoubtedly influencing it, were earlier exercises in chinoiserie forms in Europe. The chairs illustrated in fig 186, for example, are by Giuseppe Levati and came from the Villa Silva, Cinisello, near Monza, Northern Italy. They are basically neo-classical with square, straight lines and have caned seats and backs but the decoration is exceptional. The legs appear to be carved with festoon swags of drapery surmounted by lambrequin pelmets. Around the frieze of each chair is a continuous folded ribbon pattern, but the backs of the chairs contain roundels incorporating individually depicted happy Chinese boys seated in lotus position, and above and below the roundels are fan motifs. The chairs are painted in red, green, and yellow on a toned white ground.

182 With characteristic Chippendale period straight square legs, these chairs are otherwise of a bizarre pierced fretwork design, with blind fret-carving on the solid parts, and all decorated in white and gold.

*183 and 184 It is not surprising that the English admired the flowing
lines of furniture like this Louis XV chaise-longue. Fig 183 (top) shows a
pair of armchairs of about 1770, closely resembling French fauteuils, of
dancing cabriole form.*

Another remarkable set of furniture, from Bagheria, Sicily, of the late 18th century is entirely decorated with panels of verre eglomisé (decoration on glass). The sofa which is shown in fig 187 can be seen to have the glass supported by giltwood mouldings and by metal hoop patterned panels. The furniture appears to retain its original cut red velvet covering and there is a monogram in the centre of the back rail flanked on either side by helmet trophies. Conversely, another remarkable pair of white and gilt armchairs (fig 188), formerly in the collection of Count von Radetzky, owes a debt to English furniture. They were made in Sweden for the Russian market around 1785. The elegant classical linear form, strongly influenced by English and continental models, has, in addition to more conventional features, an interesting pelmeting pattern around the seat frames, scale carving on the arm supports, and an especially elegant rake to the back legs which terminate in scrolls.

Robert Adam was, as we have seen, the most notable advocate of painted furniture and he created many neo-classical masterpieces in this form. As already indicated, much furniture was conceived in close conjunction with the room in which it was placed. It is easy to imagine how the pair of tables illustrated here (fig 189) was placed within a room similarly decorated. The paintwork is in the manner of Angelica Kauffmann and Antonio Zucchi and

185 A pair of English 'bergères', a Louis XV form adapted to Robert Adam's neo-classical taste.

186 and 187 Two chairs of a wonderfully conceived chinoiserie frivolity from northern Italy; these 18th-century chairs are a foretaste of the Regency 'Indian' wonders created by the Prince Regent at Brighton Pavilion. The sofa (fig 187, below) is Sicilian incorporating decorated glass panels, verre eglomisé.

165

is of about 1790. Many familiar motifs are included and juxtaposed in the manner first adopted by Raphael and subsequently followed in the 18th century by well travelled scholars, especially Adam. Medallions and ovals depicting cupids and virtues are supported by mermaid-like arabesques, scrollings, and husks, all enclosed within a border of anthemion or honeysuckle. Other familiar motifs including urns are applied to the fronts and legs of the tables.

A very remarkable pair of giltwood armchairs in the neo-classical taste of about 1780 are further enriched with painted decoration (fig 190). The oval backs are bound with blue ribbons tied with a bow at the top and the back splats of these are also elaborately painted in the manner of Angelica Kauffmann with roundels containing ladies and cupids etc, and supported by

188 One of a notable set of white and gilt armchairs of great refinement, made in Sweden for the Russian market in about 1785.

189 (top) Neo-classical arabesques reminiscent of Raphael are a
prominent feature of one of a pair of elliptical side-tables.

190 (below) This pair of giltwood armchairs with painted decoration
linked by blue ribbons is associated with Queen Charlotte.

191 and 192 Two more pairs of Georgian armchairs, the first with shield backs and decorated in white and gold, the second (fig 192) with cobweb-shaped backs decorated like a Greek vase, in the Etruscan manner, with black and terracotta and additional white.

floral bouquets. The chairs, part of a set, one of which is in the Lady Lever Art Gallery at Port Sunlight, are associated with Queen Charlotte who reputedly worked needlework seats for them. Fragments of needlework alongside these chairs showed crowns, heraldic emblems, and flowers in knotting, laid on silk. Another fine pair of chairs (fig 191), part of a set of ten, has shield shaped backs and square tapering legs decorated in white and gold. Borders of husks moulded in *carton-pierre* (a composition) are laid along each part of the chair with a pleasingly regular effect.

Fig 194 shows a pair of armchairs with oval backs reminiscent of spiders' webs. These delicate chairs, which can be allied to George Hepplewhite's pattern book of 1788, are decorated in what is often termed the Etruscan manner. The black background is painted with motifs in terracotta, like Etruscan painting, with wonderfully delicate honeysuckle patterns in white. Classical figures fill the oval medallions in the centre of the backs. The curved 'saddle' seats are caned and would always have been fitted with squab cushions. Chairs similar to these are in the collection of H M Queen Elizabeth the Queen Mother at Clarence House, London.

I have already shown how satinwood furniture was sometimes given further painted enrichment. As a reminder of this form I include here (fig 193) a fine pair of knife boxes of the Sheraton period which are overpainted with neo-classical urns, swags, ribbon and leaf motifs, and small inset vignettes.

193 The brilliance of satinwood makes a superb ground for the painted decoration on these late 18th-century knife boxes.

CHINA, JAPAN AND INDIA

*E*ver since Marco Polo's expedition to the Far East and his discovery of China in 1275, souvenirs have been brought back to Europe. Exotic treasures, only partly understood yet full of bizarre mystery, were collected as status symbols and for their potent decorative qualities. These and the other commodities found in China were highly coveted riches. Spices, jewels, furs, porcelain, and textiles, all were laden into ships and brought home as spoils after lengthy and dangerous expeditions. By the 17th century, organised trade was well established, and by 1650 the East India Company provided London with a consistent flow of oriental exports. Soon after, arrangements were made so that orders could be placed for specific requirements in an efficient manner. Large quantities of fine textiles, woven silks, exquisite needlework, and printed and painted materials were exported to Europe. Sadly, because of their delicate nature, very many of these have perished. Better preserved are the many wonderful Chinese wallpapers which, having been brought to Europe, were safely hung around rooms on flat, upright, relatively dust-free surfaces (dust being a chief enemy, especially of textiles).

Mallett's has had several very fine examples of Chinese wallpaper. Among the most beautiful was a room of some 13 panels, all different but many of which link up in design (fig 194). The background colour is a soft blue-green and the painting depicts a delightful forest of bamboo plants in white tones

194 Part of a glorious room of Chinese wallpaper. Many variations of wall coverings in different colours and styles were imported for use in English houses during the 18th century (circa 1770).

together with a wide variety of colourful flowering and fruiting shrubs, all stemming from an undulating ground with rocky outcrops. A variety of exotic oriental butterflies and birds including pheasants and peacocks is seen perched and flying on and over the wall decoration.

The greatest of all Chinese exports was undoubtedly porcelain. Great quantities of monochrome, blue and white, and polychrome vases, large dishes, and entire services were made for the European market and shipped in large loads. Armorial services could be ordered with a family crest or coat of arms included in the decoration. In the 17th century blue and white porcelain was admired to such an extent that it was widely imitated in pottery at Delft and in England and Ireland.

Blue and white vases of large and small scale were incorporated with William and Mary furniture. A fine pair of large baluster shaped vases (fig 195), circa 1680, have eight faceted sides each differently decorated with flowering trees and flowers such as prunus, magnolia, and rhododendron. The jar tops are similarly decorated with panels containing smaller plants including bamboo shoots, and the knobs or finials have lotus leaves around them. A set of three octagonal dishes in blue and white (fig 196) of approximately the same date – the reign of K'ang Hsi – are each decorated with a central theme showing part of the pagoda scene with a gesticulating

195 From the 17th century, blue and white porcelain was imported to Europe in great quantity and featured prominently in oak panelled rooms, and alongside oriental and English lacquer.

196 (top) *Three K'ang Hsi dishes which formed part of the collection of Sir Kenelm Digby in the 17th century.*

197 (below) *A magnificent garniture of Chinese vases of large proportions, decorated with traditional landscapes. Height 28 inches.*

173

Chinaman. In the wide borders of the plates are auspicious objects linked together by a ribbon pattern. Labels on the backs of these dishes indicate that they once belonged to Sir Kenelm Digby. A garniture of five large vases dating from the middle of the 18th century (fig 197) consists of the traditional three covered jars of octagonal form and two beaker shaped vases. These are unusually decorated in coral with gilding overlaid and with reserve panels depicting polychrome landscapes and floral patterns on a white ground. The three jars with lids are surmounted by Chinese Fo dogs. A magnificent large punch bowl (fig 198) belongs to the second half of the 19th century and is of Cantonese origin. It is extremely richly decorated with flowers and insects, partly on a gilded background, with vignettes and a splendid continuous scene showing endless figures and activities.

Chinese porcelain was quickly imitated in Europe, first in pottery factories, as already mentioned, but then in many porcelain factories all over Europe. Almost as quickly the Chinese adapted to making articles to European requirements; candlesticks, teapots, and other items were made in China for export back to Europe. Another curious development was the manufacture of Canton enamel. Objects made of copper and then enamelled, in all sorts of desirable forms, including animals, teapots, boxes, vases, and candlesticks, were made in the mid-18th century countering fine European porcelain. Fig 199 shows a delightful kettle on its original heating stand. The traditionally

198 A large Cantonese punch bowl of the 19th century, profusely decorated with a continuous scene, insects, flowers and fruit.

174

white background is decorated in all colours, and includes a panel showing an interior with Chinese furniture including chairs, a table, and garden seats. A teapot of the same period (fig 200) shows European gentlemen wearing hats and drinking from beakers, sitting on mats in a distinctly Chinese landscape. A pair of exotic candlesticks are in the form of curious Chinese men as 'terms', that is, human pedestals without limbs (fig 201). In fact the arms and legs appear to be severed showing fleshy joints. Lotus flowers grow out of the Chinamen's turbans to support candles.

199 In imitation of porcelain, objects of Canton enamel were made in China for export to Europe. This tea kettle depicts an interior with interesting Chinese furniture.

Another important artistic import from China was mirror pictures. Mirror glass was always highly prized but the ultimate in decoration was a Chinese glass painted picture with mirror backing behind it. The glass was painted in reverse on the back; that is, the details were painted first, then eyelashes, faces, bodies, and landscapes, in that order. Some wonderful effects were achieved. Many of the subjects depicted included watery scenes. Two distinct varieties are particularly to be noted. Fig 202 shows the first: here, by a waterside, are elegant teal perched amongst lotus flowers and charming doves in a fruit tree. Large lotus leaves fill a significant part of the picture. The second popular design shows a landscape view. Fig 203 depicts a gentle pastoral scene where a beautifully dressed Chinese lady, holding a fly-whisk, is seated with sheep by a river while a boy plays on a pipe nearby. Also in the scene is her husband with a fine, rather small bay horse. This mirror picture retains its original elegant late-18th-century carved gilt-wood frame.

Of the abundant fine objects which we have had from Japan, many have been in the form of animals. Waterbirds seem to have played a prominent part in both Chinese and Japanese art, and amongst many splendid bronzes, sometimes of considerable scale, we have had several pairs of standing cranes. The pair shown here (fig 204) is from Japan and dates from about 1840. The birds are finely cast in bronze with shaped details on the heads and

200 and 201 Further objects of Cantonese enamel, in curious forms adapted for the European market, are decorated with European gentlemen taking tea in a Chinese landscape, and with moustached oriental torsos as supports for candles.

202 Chinese mirror paintings became a popular import to Europe. One variety traditionally depicts water birds amongst lush flowers and fruit, with silvering for the sky. Chinese, circa 1750.

203 *An elegant pastoral scene is the subject of this mid 18th-century*
Chinese mirror picture, and shows a family group at leisure by a river.
This treasured possession has been given a carved giltwood frame in
England.

204 Amongst Japanese bronze sculptures, animals and waterbirds were predominant for import to Europe. Large cranes such as these, about 6 feet high, decorated fashionable 19th-century houses and were sometimes placed in water gardens.

205 Another pair of Chinese cranes are colourfully executed in cloisonné.

in the feathering. Items such as these were frequently incorporated into water gardens or in orangeries. A smaller pair of Chinese cranes (fig 205) is of cloisonné, that is coloured enamel decoration on a brass ground and with brass filigree detailing in the enamelwork. These birds stand on roundels of stylised water and they appear to hold watersnakes under their feet.

Amongst Japanese ivory objects was this delightful duck (fig 206) of a most engaging sculptural shape and with every detail most minutely executed. Fig 207 shows a magnificent 19th-century Japanese Shibiyama carved ivory elephant encrusted with semi-precious stones and mother-of-pearl flowers. The elephant carries a huge lotus flower, and, on the underside of one foot, bears his maker's signature, Masayuki. Finally, from Japan, I show fig 208, a delightful large pair of bronze geese, finely poised and superbly executed by a craftsman who clearly felt for and understood animals.

Wonderful works of art came from India as well as from China and Japan. As artefacts from the Far East had usually been brought through India, little

206 Amongst many ivory objects, the Japanese carved domestic creatures
including this friendly duck for European patrons.

distinction was made in early times as to the exact origin of any of the imports to England. They were all described generally as 'Indian'. True Indian imports, however, were generally textiles at first. The Portuguese quickly established mercantile connections, setting up depots from which needlework, dyed and printed textiles were sent to Europe. Relatively speedily the British joined in exploiting the possibilities of setting up 'factories' for the economic manufacture of sumptuous fabrics in India. Painted and dyed 'palampores' were especially favoured for hangings, curtains, and bed-hangings. Fig 209 shows a typical and elegant example. The predominant colours were invariably a bluish red and blue, and the subjects depicted were tropical curling trees, exotic flowers, occasionally birds, and at the base a rocky undulating ground, sometimes with animals and figures.

A certain amount of Indian-made furniture found its way to Europe in special circumstances, and also at home English furniture was made of imported Indian wood. The very magnificent Chippendale period cabinet of

207 (opposite, above) Bejewelled ivory elephants were brought to England from Japan as one of the treasures of the East.

208 (opposite, below) A pair of sensitively sculptured Japanese bronze geese, circa 1840.

209 (above) Indian textiles played a prominent part in English furnishings. Palampores such as this were incorporated as hangings for walls and beds.

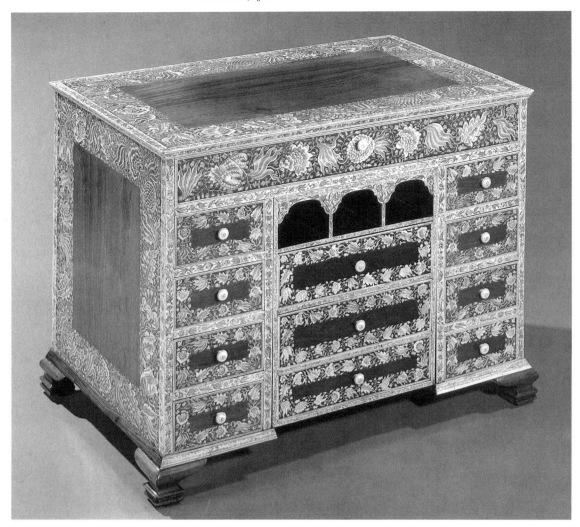

padouk which is illustrated on page 119 (fig 133) is an important example. Padouk is a kind of rosewood with fairly prominent markings and of a lovely warm colour.

Ivory was of course a principal treasure and to be found plentifully in India. Although we now deplore the hunting of elephants, it must be remembered that in the 18th and 19th centuries, and indeed until relatively recently, elephants were very numerous as their vast habitat had not been reduced. Sad as it is to think of these noble animals being hunted for their tusks they were by no means rare then, as they are today. Furniture made with ivory ornament or of solid ivory was very popular and a surprising amount of it has survived. Furniture made at Vizagatapatam for the European market was usually of padouk or rosewood with ivory inlay. The soft tones of the mellow wood resembling light mahogany blended well with the delicate floral ivory inlay that was painstakingly etched with detailing. Fig 210 shows a magnificent large knee-hole desk with three central drawers and pigeon-holes. The centre may be pulled forward or pushed back to allow

210 Ivory furniture from several parts of India was made when the material was not scarce. This desk was made in Vizagatapatam, southern India, circa 1770.

for knee space. The choice of flowers and leaves in the bands of decoration is closely associated with the exotic plants represented in the textiles that had been popular for so long.

A very remarkable set of solid ivory chairs associated with Warren Hastings is shown in fig 211. With tigers' heads on the arm supports and gilt decoration added to the carving, these and a few similar chairs are said to have belonged to Tipu Sultan of Mysore. Another delightful pair of solid ivory armchairs (fig 212) is conceived entirely in the European manner and is of particularly elegant, Hepplewhite-influenced design. Of tub chair form with triple splat backs and standing on delicate tapered legs, all richly decorated with gilt patterns, the chairs are an extraordinary and happy combination of Anglo-Indian synthesis. Fig 213 is perhaps less elegant but still very remarkable. Dating probably from the early 19th century, this solid ivory chair is in many respects a more refined version of 17th-century Portuguese ebony furniture. Another remarkable specimen piece is the curvilinear armchair shown in fig 214. Apparently inspired by the bentwood

211 A magnificent pair of solid ivory armchairs, part of a set of seat furniture said to have belonged to Warren Hastings, who seized it from Tipu Sultan of Mysore in 1799.

furniture of Thonet of Austria, this superb piece is of solid ivory, beautifully worked with minute gold damascene inlay on every surface. Only the frame of the seat and the stretcher support are not of solid ivory.

A wonderful Indian object which was to be seen in the shop some years ago is an 18th-century ivory howdah (fig 215), of boat shape with canted corners. Solid pieces of ivory which must have been taken from colossal tusks are used in shaped panels, carefully pegged together and supported by a few metal brackets. This wonderful elephant-borne throne, which would have been further enriched with sumptuous velvet upholstery or silk cushions, must have been made for a Moghul Prince, perhaps a Maharajah. A similar patron must have been responsible for the even more opulent though considerably later silver howdah of fig 216. This huge piece could only have been placed on a very large elephant. Solid beaten silver shaped into a fascinating form is laid over a wooden framework in exactly the same manner as the baroque silver furniture mentioned at the beginning of this book (see page 21).

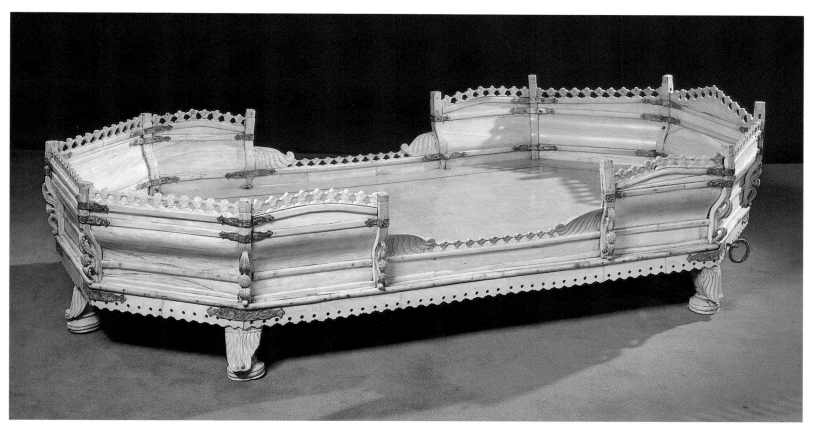

212 (opposite, above) Chairs of solid ivory with gilded decoration. The elegant forms were presumably copied directly from English chairs taken to India.

213 (opposite, below left) Another Indian ivory armchair, with caned seat and back, and with turned legs and other decoration more traditionally Indo-Portuguese.

214 (opposite, below right) A remarkable Caucasian chair, with curling lines painstakingly formed from ivory, and intricately inlaid with gold damascene.

215 (above) This Moghul howdah of solid ivory panels, carefully shaped and pegged together, must have been furnished with fine textiles and been borne by a rich caparisoned elephant.

Tigers are the principal symbol adorning this howdah, protecting the ends of the seats and surrounding, on the front, a large Surya sun motif.

Indian jewellery is a relatively new specialisation at Bourdon House. Amongst very fine tribal and courtly jewellery, some is relatively ethnic in design while other pieces are seen to follow the Moghul, chiefly Islamic tradition. Fig 217 shows a group of remarkable gold necklaces. The largest piece is a magnificent 18th-century necklace in the form of one hundred stylised jasmine flowers linked by small rubies to a running floriate border. This is from Tamil Nadu, southern India. Two central necklaces are of the 19th century while a gold coat of arms hangs from a chain of gold links and carved rudrak nuts. This is also from Tamil Nadu, and dates from about 1880.

216 Imagine the massive elephant that bore this large and heavy silver howdah, which has protective tigers and a sun god motif in its decoration.

217 A group of Tamil gold necklaces from southern India displays
strange but fascinating sophistication.

TEXTILES

Textiles, perhaps, were even more important than furniture in the fitting out of interiors. Indeed in early inventories the word 'furniture' refers not to wooden pieces but to textiles and soft furnishings in general. They were amongst the most valuable possessions a man might own, and early wills often opened with bequests of very highly valued beds, complete with treasured hangings. Lavish textiles – sumptuous silks, velvets, damask, tapestries, and needlework – were a high status symbol in household furnishing. Sadly only a tiny faction of these have survived, since they are extremely fragile and prone to rotting through light damage and destruction by moth. As fashions changed and as pieces became worn, textiles were adapted from one use to another, often ending up, as they do too frequently today, in the form of cushions which are inevitably even more quickly worn out.

However, a remarkable number of splendid specimens has survived. 17th-century needlework panels, framed and glazed, are preserved in great numbers and indeed huge quantities of these must have been made by almost every young girl who would become literate. During the first 15 years of life, these girls might be expected to work several samplers, a picture or two – perhaps one in beadwork – and possibly a needlework box. They would then be prepared for the duties of womanhood; capable of marking linen, of

218 Mallett's were especially delighted when a generous donor acquired an outstanding set of needlework furniture in order to return it to Canons Ashby, for which it was made in the early 18th century.

sewing and embroidering costume, and in some cases, of carrying out other grander artistic works such as making bed hangings or working on embroidered panels of considerable scale. A fine stumpwork mirror has already been shown (see fig 15, page 28). Similar themes, of pattern-book origin, as depicted in that piece were repeated over and over again in slightly different combinations. A very fine panel of beadwork (fig 219) of about 1669 shows in the centre a representation of one of the senses – smell – as a lady holding a flower. Around her are placed numerous sprigs, flowers, birds, insects, and animals including a stag and a camel. A huge tulip is placed at one side and a lily opposite, and above, the sun shines from multi-coloured clouds. The background of the picture, which is worked on silk, is powdered all over with small pieces of mother-of-pearl and the picture is signed in pearls with the initials E.L. Fig 220, a needlework picture of few decades later, shows Abraham about to sacrifice Isaac. The event never happened of course and the substitute ram is seen miraculously caught in a briar nearby. A wonderful variety of other animals derived from a bestiary is depicted together with numerous flowers, insects, and creatures in a hillocky landscape. Note also the splendid cupid-like angel calling to Abraham from the clouds.

Sets of crewelwork bed curtains made entirely of homegrown wool and

219 A late 17th-century beadwork picture retains the bright colour that so much needlework must have had originally. We have become accustomed to more muted tones.

worked by amateurs and professionals alike to exotic designs closely associated with Indian palampores (see fig 209) were made in considerable quantities in the late 17th and 18th centuries. Earlier ones were usually in tones of blue-green with a few added details in other colours. In the 18th century they became much lighter in design and very much more colourful. An extremely rare set of curtains (fig 224) of about 1700, are of flame colours, with red, yellow, orange, and darker shadings. A regular design of winding trees, exotic flowers, and leaves, stems from an undulating ground. The curtains are entirely worked in wool on linen twill.

A small but magnificent needlework picture of about 1710 (fig 221) is worked in silk, entirely in rococo stitch and with a background of white in diaper pattern. Another fine panel of about 1750 may once have been made for a fire screen. Entirely of needlework and worked in wools with silk highlights, like a Dutch still life it shows a wide variety of flowers stemming from a vase, with a snail below (fig 222).

Mallett's was closely associated with Dr Douglas Goodhart in the formation of his magnificent collection of fine 17th-century samplers which are now to be seen at Montacute House, Somerset. We have also had some very fine 18th-century samplers. A pretty one of 1799 by Elizabeth Wright is

220 The gruesome near-slaughter of Isaac is set amidst a bestiary of animals derived from pattern books in this 17th-century needlework picture.

221 (top) Remarkably fresh colours are combined with beautiful stitching in this early 18th-century needlework picture.

222 (above left) Many English needlework panels, displaying a variety of flowers in a vase, were ultimately derived from Dutch still-life paintings.

223 (above right) Making samplers trained young girls in both sewing and their alphabets. This one is dated 1799.

shown here (fig 223). Within a characteristic border, letters, numbers, and a text are combined with repeated motifs of flowers and animals and the eight-year-old girl's signature.

Furniture was frequently enriched with splendid textiles. Beds were hung with lavish curtains of velvet or needlework and seat furniture was often upholstered and covered with fine fabrics. A magnificent example of the union of furniture and needlework is represented by a suite of walnut furniture that Mallett's discovered recently and saw restored to its original home at Canons Ashby, Northamptonshire (owned by the National Trust), through a generous benefaction. The furniture consists of a sofa, six side-chairs and a fire screen, all of walnut and all with particularly fine needlework. Gervase Jackson-Stops has identified these in the accounts of the house as a purchase from a maker who was prominent in his day but who is unknown to us now. Thomas Phill was recorded in 1719 at the sign of The Three Golden Chairs in the Strand. His bill of five years earlier indicated that he supplied Edward Dryden of Canons Ashby with six walnut back chair frames 'of the newest fashion' with green serge for the backs and gold serge for false cases. He also charged 'ffor making ye needlework covers and fixeing ym on ye chaires' (fig 218). The design of the needlework on each chair seat and back shows a bouquet of multicoloured flowers, still wonderfully preserved, stemming from a single blue and white vase against a white background. They are astonishingly beautiful, as are also the sofa and screen. The sofa's needlework depicts two scenes with figures within an overall floral design.

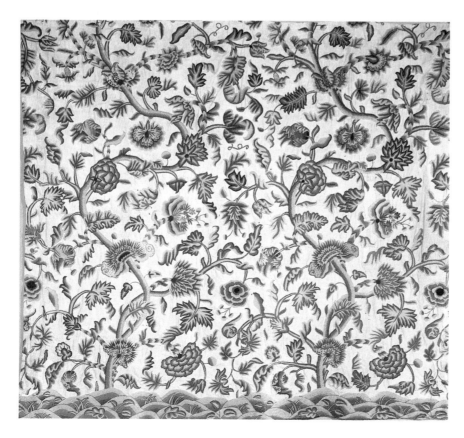

224 An English crewelwork curtain of about 1700, embroidered in flame-coloured wools, owes more than a little to Indian painted and embroidered cottons.

A MISCELLANY

OF WONDERFUL

OBJECTS

*L*et us now consider a number of objects, each rather special, some even unique, not easy to categorize within normal furniture development, but all reflecting aspects of quality. They demonstrate the Georgian abilities to create utilitarian objects in a naturally artistic way, and also to conceive artistic objects with an extremely tenuous utilitarian excuse. First we may look at a piece of furniture: a gigantic mirror (fig 226) 11ft high, entirely framed in engraved glass with superb heraldic trophies. Every part of the border and scrolled cresting is engraved with symbols of war and peace, or at any rate, victory. Colossal fanfares of banners are interspersed with prancing horses and trophies of battle equipment. This *tour de force* of glass engraving was made in Germany in the early 18th century. The mirror was acquired by us from Mentmore Towers, Buckinghamshire when Lord Rosebery's great Rothschild collection was dispersed in 1977.

Totally different, though still in the glass world, is a magnificent collection of Dutch engraved glass which we exhibited in 1990. Amongst 45 outstanding items were examples of diamond, wheel, and stipple engraved glasses, some of them unique historic pieces. Included was a tall glass flute, 15 inches high, circa 1660, engraved with a portrait of the five-year-old Prince William of Orange seated on a prancing horse (fig 227). It was this prince who in 1677 married Princess Mary, eldest daughter of James II of

225 That these 18th-century lead garden figures were over-painted regularly meant the extraordinary preservation of their original colour decoration (see page 209).

England and Scotland, and became King William III of England; and it was this partnership that was crowned King and Queen of England and Scotland in 1689 (see page 19).

Of the first half of the 18th century is an extremely rare set of four glass candlesticks (fig 228) with inverted Silesian stems, domed bases, and moulded sconces. A splendid large Queen Anne brass porringer with cover, engraved with the arms of the Jopp family of Hampshire, has a certain comfortable bulk reminiscent of earlier decades but also a delightful simplicity of decoration (fig 229).

Heraldry is the most satisfactory and continuously suitable of all forms of ornament. It is historic, meaningful, and beautiful; its language carries forward in arms interesting information of personal involvement and links between families, towns, institutions and nations. A walk around the cloisters of Winchester Cathedral viewing the bosses in the vaulted ceiling or noting the arms in needlework firescreens in country houses both tell of people of the day who were involved in building up of all that is about us. A superb pair of mid-18th-century brass wine coolers are also engraved with shields and coronets; the linking of two escutcheons may commemorate a marriage. These are shown on the lacquer chest in fig 65.

226 (opposite) A colossal German mirror presents a tour de force of 18th-century glass engraving.

227 (above left) The future William III of England is engraved on this rare survival, a Dutch flute for drinking red wine.

228 (above) A set of four delightful early 18th-century glass candlesticks.

*229 Heraldry provides the only ornament on this elegantly shaped brass
porringer, as on so much 17th-century silver.*

*230 A pair of late 18th-century commodes entirely veneered in turtle
shell, with a coloured foil behind to give it a deeper tone.*

Returning to furniture I now show a rarity and curiosity. This is a remarkable pair of half-round commodes (fig 230), English circa 1770. They are entirely veneered with tortoiseshell or, more correctly, turtle-shell as the pieces are of a large size. This material is fixed on with a foil behind it in order to lighten the colour and show up the markings.

Marie Antoinette delighted in affecting characteristics of the life of a country maid; she liked to play at being a dairy girl with porcelain pails and to display the appropriate utensils and costume of a frivolous rustic nature. The elegant English mahogany and brass spinning wheel (fig 231) is certainly a utilitarian object but of a quality which suggests that it was made for well-bred hands. A brass label on it bears the inscription 'S. Thorp of Abberley'. A full-sized harp (fig 232) was also clearly made for a lady (or possibly a man) of high rank since it is elaborately decorated with a carved giltwood cresting and the framework is entirely japanned. Even the soundboard is painted with a series of chinoiserie figures. Fig 233 shows a sedan chair of about 1780 which is said to have belonged to Lady Liverpool. The polished black leather on the outside with panels of red is overlaid with bands of classical ornament: scrolls, swags of husks, a crowned monogram, and tassels, all in repoussé metal. The top is surmounted by a coronet.

Tea was a tremendously precious commodity in 18th-century England and, along with spices, was a precious import from China. It was invariably kept

231 and 232 Georgian elegance and quality is here applied to a mundane spinning-wheel; and the noble pursuit of playing the harp is celebrated in a fine instrument decorated with carving and chinoiserie painting.

*233 Lady Liverpool's sedan chair is of black and red leather, decorated
with embossed metalwork.*

under lock and key. This treasured substance gave rise to the manufacture of many wonderful tea services. Tea caddies, tea sets, silver and porcelain, for use in tea drinking were all part of a fashion which became something of a ceremony and still is almost a religious habit of English people today. Very many small boxes of superb quality were made to contain tea in all materials, silver, wood, ivory, tortoishell, rolled paper, and even glass. The study of wooden ones shows a microcosm of the history of 18th-century craftsmanship. A particularly charming fashion was to make wooden tea caddies in the form of fruit including pears, apples, melons, and very occasionally, pineapples (fig 234). These caddies were usually made of close grained fruitwood and colour would be added to the wood to represent realistic red and green tones. These colours have invariably now faded leaving a delightful patina and variety of shades. The caddies often retained their original locks and keys and were lined on the interior with foil which was intended to protect the freshness of the tea leaves. An unusual and

234 Ever a precious commodity, tea was kept locked in these fruit-shaped caddies which were tinted with realistic colours.

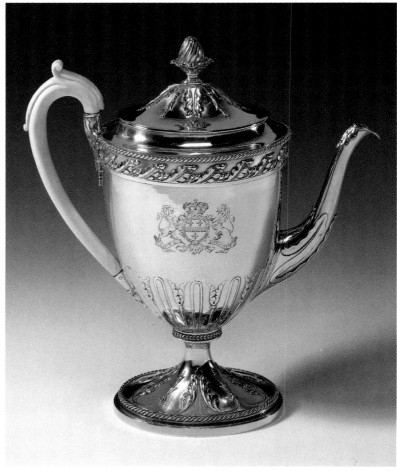

beautiful Russian tea caddy with faceted sides was entirely decorated with polished and cut steel. It also had ivory bandings and was inset with painted miniatures showing theatrical scenes. It was made in about 1780. A splendid silver tea set (fig 235) circa 1770 consists of two silver tea caddies, a tea pot, a dozen spoons, and sugar tongs. The larger pieces are engraved with the arms and initials of Morris Moore of Mooresfoot, County Tipperary, and all are set in a case lined with velvet and veneered with green shagreen (ray rather than jackass in this case) with silver mounts. In magnificent silver gilt with an ivory handle is a fine coffee pot of 1797 by Paul Storr. This elegant piece is entirely representative of the best silver of the period. Again, it is labelled with arms and supporters (fig 236).

Curious and unique is a box made for containing a Stilton cheese (fig 237). This circular, mahogany container is in two halves, opening to reveal a lead lining. The cheese is kept aired by ivory portholes with spindle fenestration to keep out mice and is surmounted by a large brass finial. Castors with leather treads allow the piece to be wheeled around the table. Used for the same purpose as the brass wine cooler of fig 262 is a splendid pair of English mid-18th-century mahogany ones with brass bindings and handles. These are

235 The ceremony of drinking tea was heightened by the use of luxurious utensils. This silver tea set is fitted in a shagreen case.

236 Paul Storr made this silver-gilt coffee-pot in 1797.

237 A Georgian caddy, on wheels, for a Stilton cheese, and a pair of lined ice-buckets to cool bottles of hock, both of mahogany and circa 1780.

206

made to contain a single bottle but zinc linings beneath the removable rims at the top contain compartments for ice to cool the wine.

Gardens present another opportunity for delight and luxury, and urns and statues of stone or lead were made to punctuate embroidered carpets of flowers and hooded yew hedges, like hangings. A poetic delight in Arcadia is seen in many forms of 18th-century art, and rustic activities were alluded to and depicted in every medium. Shepherds and shepherdesses were often shown in idyllic settings, never at work, but languidly contemplating their simple and happy life. They appear in every substance, in porcelain and needlework especially. Their sheep turn up on giltwood mirrors, while they themselves are also found in garden statuary. A charming pair of lead figures (fig 225) is attributed to John Cheere (1709-87), who had workshops at Hyde Park Corner and who produced quantities of decorative rococo sculpture in various materials. His brother Sir Henry Cheere was already famed for his marble sculpture, and is represented by monumental works in Westminster Abbey. These figures, standing 56 inches high, retain most of the original polychrome decoration that disguised the relatively inexpensive lead. This paintwork had been covered (and protected) by many layers of later painting. When these were removed, the original colours were discovered and it was fortunately possible to save them. A particularly fine pair of composition stone figures (fig 238) presents a sporting couple. A young man primes his gun, filling the barrel with gun powder and shot. His female companion, in elegant country costume and a hat, holds dead game.

While it could be argued that the finest clock makers, famed for wonderful movements, flowered towards the end of the 17th century and at the beginning of the 18th century, it is equally true to say that superlative cases for good clocks were made during the second half of the 18th century. A splendid variation of the traditional in bracket clocks is seen in fig 239, where the case is entirely covered with mirrored glass with engraved decoration. The silver of this, together with the gilt spandrels on the front and other gilt mounts including embossed sound panels at the sides and a balustrade around the top, present a very rich effect. This might have been made for the Turkish market, as certainly was the clock by George Prior of London in fig 240 which has Arabic numerals on the face. In this instance, the case is veneered with tortoishell and lined with red foil. This is contrasted with ormolu mounts including pierced plates to allow the sound of bells to be heard.

Fig 242 shows an outstanding ormolu clock which must have been made by the great metalsmith, Matthew Boulton (1728-1802), as it exactly resembles in form a wonderful clock made for George III to a design by Sir William

238 A pair of stone garden figures in the form of a refined sporting couple, elegantly dressed (English, circa 1790).

Chambers which is still in the royal collection. The two clocks have slight differences. In this example there is a plinth of blue-john, or Derbyshire fluorspar, supporting the urn at the top while around the face of the clock there is a panel of blue painted glass. Mallett's sold this clock some years ago and more recently it has been acquired from Messrs Hotspur by the Courtauld Institute for Somerset House. The superbly strong, almost exaggerated, neo-classical features which are a characteristic of some of Sir William Chambers' finest architecture are wonderfully carried out in this magnificent piece of metalwork. Huge swags of laurel leaves are draped from rams' heads, and above these are four finials in the form of large ewers.

Objets de vertu from France were prominent amongst an English gentleman's possessions, and included with these were fine clocks of marble and ormolu. Two French clocks of much the same period, that is 1780, have similar movements and round enamel faces. They have very different cases, however, each of an upright, perpendicular nature, perhaps designed to be placed between a pair of sympathetic objects on a mantelpiece or commode top. One (fig 243) is in a chinoiserie setting, enclosed in a pagoda crowned with a Chinaman seated beneath a parasol and resting on the roof of a pavilion which has four dragons at the corners. Within the pavilion is a

239 and 240 Clocks have often been princely treasures and been given rich cases. These examples show one of mirrored glass and another of tortoiseshell, with arabic numerals suitable for the Turkish market.

group of chinoiserie figures, executed in biscuit porcelain, enclosed within an ormolu fence with bells hanging above. The second clock (fig 241) is in neo-classical form set within a trophy of arms presented by a pair of cupids, all in ormolu of finely chiselled quality. This composition rests at the top of a classical arch with a marble top and base and encloses a fine pendulum in the form of a sunburst with Apollo's mask at the centre.

A much more restrained but also very elegant shelf or table clock has a movement by Vulliamy of London, circa 1810, and is in a tall satinwood case with a splayed base. A dial on the side sets the bells to sound or be silent. The woodwork is ornamented with gilt brass rams' heads, a pineapple finial, a bezel around the face, and four ball feet. The clock is shown on the library table illustrated in fig 258.

The Matthew Boulton clock leads us to three items all attributed to Boulton's workshop. The first is a pair of candelabra (fig 244) in the form of blue-john urns wonderfully elegantly overlaid with gilt mounts, both having a pair of candle sconce arms on either side. The egg-shaped pieces of blue-john rest on spiral turned bases. Another magnificent single blue-john urn (fig 245) is in the form of a classical vase with a cover. It stands on double plinths also of that semi-precious stone. The ormolu is of the highest quality and has

241 and 242 This clock case is of identical form to one made by Matthew Boulton for George III; while fig 241 shows a French clock of the same period with another fine ormolu setting.

243 Clocks are often mounted in architectural cases. This chinoiserie pagoda contains a biscuit porcelain group, and is dripping with ormolu fantasies.

wonderfully rich gilding. Animal masks in leafy cartouches adorn the four sides of the urn while one plinth is supported by four sphinxes and garlanded, and the other is encased within scrolling tendrils and flowers. Thirdly, I illustrate a magnificent large pair of tôle knife boxes (fig 247) attributed to Matthew Boulton, in the form of egg-shaped urns. These contain fitments for cutlery. They are of metal painted in simulation of porphyry, mounted with neo-classical fittings in the form of medallions, swags, lion-mask ring handles, scroll bandings and finials.

Amongst fine English porcelain must be mentioned a very magnificent pair of covered tureens (fig 246) which form part of the Stowe Service. These were made for the second Marquess of Buckingham at the Flight, Barr and Barr factory at Worcester in 1813. The arms are superbly painted and the richness of the gilt decoration on a beige ground is outstanding.

244 Matthew Boulton provided the ormolu mounts for the Derbyshire fluorspar urns at the centre of these candelabra (circa 1780).

245 Another perfect combination of blue-john (fluorspar) with gilt
mounts, by Matthew Boulton.

246 A pair of tureens, from the Stowe service made for the Marquess of
Buckingham at Worcester in 1813.

247 *These comfortable egg-shaped knife boxes, attributed to Matthew Boulton, are of tôle, decorated to look like porphyry. They have ormolu mounts and the lids rise on a spring rachet.*

Returning to furniture, I would like to mention three interesting but not easily classifiable items. Firstly we have a tavern chair or Windsor armchair dating from the first half of the 18th century (fig 248). Made, unusually, of walnut, this must be a rare survival of a once plentiful type of furniture, the vast majority having been broken or considered not worthy of preservation. The low back with its central vase-shaped splat and upright rungs is classic Windsor chair form, as is the saddle-shaped solid seat. This is frequently made of ash where other parts of the chair are of the more pliable yew. The arm supports here are carved in scroll form. The chair stands on a combination of cabriole legs at the front and straight legs at the back, the two kinds joined by stretchers.

Next we have a three seater sofa (fig 250) in Windsor chair form. This is an extremely rare model, especially since the yew wood back is pierced in gothic fashion echoing the arched outline of the chairback. Refined cabriole legs with corner brackets, and turned legs at the back, are joined by hoop stretchers designed, it is sometimes said, to allow for crinoline skirts. Also gothic but in a classical vein is this pair of late 18th-century mahogany hall side-chairs (fig 249). The pedimented backs are indented with bas relief gothic arches while a medieval trefoil pattern fills the tympanum above. The front legs, however, are of a curious flattened cabriole form, leaning towards neo-classicism with acanthus leaves at the knees and terminating in claw feet.

248 Rustic elegance is captured in this 18th-century tavern chair of walnut.

249 and 250 (opposite) Sophisticated gothic arches are incorporated in a pair of neo-classical mahogany hall chairs of about 1800; while true gothic arches and piercing are formed in yew wood in a splendid three-seater 18th-century bench.

Finally, a series of four chandeliers represents the span of the Georgian age. The first is one of a pair of magnificent George I giltwood chandeliers with gilt lead mounts that came from Holme Lacey, Herefordshire. This I have already illustrated (see page 82, fig 86). Also George I is a magnificent double tier brass chandelier. This one (fig 251) has sconces for 20 candles, the arms of which are fitted into a tall central stem with bulbous elements, and having gadrooned domes at the top and bottom. Chippendale period giltwood chandeliers have seldom survived but an especially fine one attributed to Mathias Lock is shown in fig 101 on page 93. This chandelier dates from around 1760. By the third quarter of the 18th century, nothing was more fashionable than elegant cut glass chandeliers of icy crispness, sometimes augmented with simple gilt bands on the central stem. The magnificent one illustrated (fig 252) is said to have been made for the Russian market but more recently came from Ditchley Park, Oxfordshire. Twelve noble 's' shaped arms stem from a central cut glass bowl with a large urn above it and inverted bowls at the top and bottom, hung with faceted drops to catch the light. Other swags of drops hang delicately to create a web of diamond-like glitter.

251 Magnificent 17th- and 18th-century brass chandeliers such as this one are still to be seen in some churches.

252 (opposite) Even more than polished brass, later cut-glass chandeliers sparkled and reflected light like bejewelled coronets.

Mallett's has always delighted in curious and unusual objects when they are also beautiful and well made. We have had a wide variety of strange things in the shop, often placed neatly on a specially made plinth or stand covered in one of our silk velvets. At first sight these might seem somewhat at odds with the traditional furniture in our galleries which on the whole conforms to a recognisable historical progression. But these unusual objects also reflect the luxurious craftsmanship of past generations and represent specially fascinating by-ways of idiosyncratic excellence. We particularly like to notice relatively normal artefacts made with unusual artistic quality.

A charming collection of 61 19th-century fishing reels (fig 253) took its place happily amongst mahogany and lacquer furniture some years ago. These reels, chiefly of brass, but also silver and wood, were each superbly made and finished with simple and practical decoration. Carefully assembled by some enthusiast, the group is arranged in spiral form on a wall panel. It is fun to consider the fishing exploits that the reels must have witnessed and

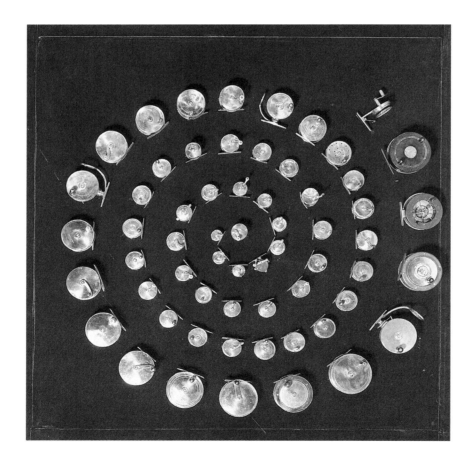

253 An interesting collection of 19th-century brass fishing reels.

now, past useful requirement, they are saved and enjoyed as a general ornament and part of angling history.

Small wooden objects, boxes etc are often known as treen. Turning is sometimes a feature of such pieces. An especially interesting item of treen is the egg cup stand in fig 254, most painstakingly made of contrasting dark and light woods and with rims and other elements in ivory. In two tiers the stand holds a set of 12 egg cups and below these hang spoons in ivory brackets. Whether this was one of a number of pieces made by a craftsman, or a sole fantasy, or even a special order, is not known but it is certainly likely to be a sole survivor after perhaps 200 years.

254 Treen: an elaborate egg cup stand made in contrasting woods with turned ivory mouldings (circa 1800).

Another special and elegant dining-room item is a rare pair of boat-shaped wine coasters (fig 255) of red Morocco leather. Each boat contains a pair of round holders with elegant pear shaped glass decanters. Charming silver labels hanging on the decanters mark them for Claret, Hock, Champagne, and Vindegrave. These and the silver trimmings on the coasters are all hallmarked London 1796, and made by Phipps and Robinson. The leather is stamped Hardwick, No 463 Strand.

Another little group of luxuries (fig 256) includes a silver gilt inkwell in the form of a tortoise. The shell folds open to reveal bottles and a space for pen nibs. The pair of octagonal tea caddies and the two photograph frames are of tortoiseshell with ivory and silver gilt details respectively.

A spectacular extravagance that must be unique is a baby carriage said to have been made for the Duke of Wellington to be used by his eldest son, Viscount Douro (fig 257). This delightful vehicle, on three wheels, is carved in the form of an open giltwood shell, fitted with a seat, with gilt bronze mounts, and it bears a coronet and the initial D.

255 These leather coasters are trimmed with silver mounts of 1796, and the wine labels for the elegant decanters were provided at the same time.

256 (opposite, above) A group of late 19th-century luxuries, including a silver gilt inkwell in the form of a tortoise.

257 (opposite, below) This baby carriage was commissioned by the Duke of Wellington for his son. The seat is contained within a carved and silvered shell.

THE NINETEENTH CENTURY

The 19th century was not an age of gracefulness. While Georgian characteristics were continued in some respects, there was a general coarsening of style as the decades went by and an increasing development of ornateness based on a number of earlier styles. The Victorian traits of sentimentality, clutter, and muddled scholasticism, were gathering force with considerable momentum. Despite this gloomy generalisation about a one-hundred-year period, there were, of course, some true artists and wonderful works were created. In the world of interior decoration there is no doubt that new forms of room layout for specific requirements were conceived as part of a new taste and fashion. But to our eyes, perhaps more in sympathy with neo-Georgianism at present, much of the 19th century seems over-charged, unnecessarily complicated, and lacking elegance or originality.

The first three decades are effectively embraced within the term 'Regency'; George IV actually became Prince Regent in 1811 and succeeded his father as King in 1820. During this period the neo-classicism that had dominated the last part of the 18th century was extended to new limits much more extreme in design and highly original. Instead of a revival of only Greek and Roman motifs, designs were based on a broader language of classical metaphor which included these, together with Etruscan and, most important of all, Egyptian idioms. The campaigns and expeditions of Napoleon, Nelson,

258 The elegant lines of an early Regency library table in the manner of Henry Holland provide a large surface for folios, and here for a pair of early 18th-century table globes (see page 209) and a clock by William Vulliamy.

Wellington and others, inspired a general interest in new parts of the world, especially Egypt, and it became fashionable to make studies of Egyptian culture. Thomas Hope (1767-1831) was foremost in advocating a new clarity of design that was wholly original but clearly based on a revival of elements of Greek, Roman, and Egyptian civilisation. Motifs and forms from each were included in his *Household Furniture and Interior Decoration* of 1807. In this work, a somewhat scholarly approach is adapted to become a captivating novelty. Of work carried out in his own London house it was said it would 'contribute to emancipate the public taste'. He was certainly the most significant designer of the high Regency period.

From the 1830s on, there were many revivals running upon each other so fast that they sometimes combined happily, but on other occasions led to confusing, mixed designs, clearly derivative and not with enough strength or originality to stand as properly developed styles. Revivals and adaptations of Italian Renaissance and medieval Gothic by Gilbert Scott and Pugin had considerable influence, first in architecture, but were soon taken up by other enthusiasts and, unfortunately, quickly coarsened. There was a lack of unified feeling and direction clouding many aspects of interest, though nuggets of success are always to be found.

The productivity of the middle decades of the 19th century was enormous, stimulated by the huge demand of an ever increasing number of patrons who had sufficient money and a desire to establish great houses using the fortunes which they had recently built up. This colossal wealth was the result of British enterprise in the colonies, the empire-building which brought a considerable economic bonanza.

In the meantime the industrial revolution led to the growth of many new fortunes at home and an overall increase in the spending power of a rising upper middle-class with patrons who were potential builders of houses. These new rich wished to create fine homes fully furnished and equipped with the luxury fittings and furniture which they saw as suitable to their status. They sometimes sought for a traditional appearance, and in this respect, the fashion for antiquarianism and revivals of the old styles – Greek, Roman, Egyptian, Renaissance, Gothic etc – fitted in admirably. Many were industrialists and entrepreneurs busy creating and increasing their fortunes. They were not usually the aristocratic patrons of the 18th century who found time to be serious students of art and architecture, going to Italy on the 'grand tour' in order to witness and participate in the creation of the fashionable neo-classical style. Yet in the new England of money-making and castle building there was room for expression and feeling, and when this was shown honestly it could be very satisfactory.

The less good side however, led to Victorian sentimentality and a terrible overdose of ornament and gloom. This sickly characteristic seems to me to be emotional hypocrisy, showing up, in fact, the gross injustices in society. A kind of cover-up and show of humility reflecting a two-facedness and the less good aspects of strong imperialism and tough, successful industrialisation.

Real artists, however, were fully grounded in history, literature, and art and sought to create something permanent out of their close study and knowledge of artistic backgrounds. William Morris (1834-1896) especially tried to understand medieval, Islamic, and other early art and craftsmanship; he was particularly determined to counteract the broad tidal wave of industrial manufacture and to ensure that works of art were given the highest possible quality in handmade craftsmanship and personal attention. Like the great painters, Turner and Samuel Palmer, he hoped to develop new forms

259 An elegant rosewood writing and reading table, with a leather top and brass and gilded mouldings (circa 1800).

that would grow naturally out of earlier styles but at the same time reflect a degree of ancestry and background. Sometimes the search for purity led to a certain austerity, a kind of academic overdose of revival, weighty and scholastic, a bit too serious from an artistic point of view and certainly not decorative in our understanding of the word. It sometimes tended to display knowledge rather than cloak wisdom within creative decoration, and lacked a natural warmth.

The earlier part of the Regency period maintains many of the elegant characteristics of late 18th-century furniture. We see a considerable use of light coloured woods as favoured by Sheraton and of pieces of furniture with straight lines, simply ornamented with reeding, cross-banding, and line inlay. Holland (1746-1806) was an architect who worked for the Prince of Wales (later George IV) at Carlton House. He was instrumental in introducing Graeco-Roman detail in England, but much furniture associated with his name has a relative simplicity of line. A splendid large satinwood library or gallery table (fig 258, page 222) with a leather top and a large stretcher in the form of a shelf below, possibly used to rest books on, is attributed to Henry Holland. Mouldings of mahogany and cross-bandings and lines are contrasted with satinwood veneers. The piece stands on eight slender, tapering, reeded legs which rest on large brass castors.

Also with 18th-century proportions is a fine writing table (fig 259) quite probably made by John Maclean who became known for fine furniture of rosewood with brass mounts in the form of mouldings, lions' heads, and a louvre panel motif. This splendid piece contains in the top a book-rest on a

260 A pair of cabinets, with figured mahogany doors framed with satinwood, and with agate tops.

ratchet support. The shape of the table is that of a sofa table, with single end supports standing on splayed legs joined by a turned stretcher. The top is lined with leather. A delightful pair of commodes (fig 260) are in a most restrained rectangular form but are richly decorated with very fine mahogany and satinwood veneers which are framed within bandings and mouldings of very fine quality gilt metal. Unusual agate-type marble tops complement the fine figuring of the mahogany panels in the doors. A small desk (fig 261) is of the kind known as a 'davenport' (after Gillows supplied a certain 'Captain Davenport' a desk); it is of rosewood with drawers in one side and dummy handles on the others. There is a slide under the writing section which itself is on runners so that it can be pulled forward to provide a knee-hole under the sloping top. Rosewood became very popular in England in the Regency period. It was imported from Brazil and the East Indies. It is basically a rather dark wood with strong markings but is especially attractive when it is somewhat bleached or faded.

261 An early 19th-century desk known as a davenport. Of rosewood, it has a sliding top section, slides and drawers in one side.

Mahogany, however, remained an important material for furniture making and the finest pieces, even if veneered with other woods, would usually be made partly of mahogany. A brass bound container on a stand in rectangular form with canted corners and with brass lions' head mask handles at each end (fig 262) is in this case used as a jardinière, but its original purpose was for cooling wine. Lined with lead, the container was waterproof to hold bottles and ice. A fine pair of library armchairs (fig 263) are of mahogany with carved seats, backs and sides. These are fitted with leather squab cushions and armpads. Fitted to the arms is a swinging bookrest and candle sconce. The chairs are of a comfortable, classical design with turned legs and may well have been designed by Henry Holland or supplied by Gillows of Lancaster. A delightful set of four Regency armchairs (fig 265) are closely related to a design by Sheraton in his *Cabinet-maker and Upholsterer's Drawing book*. They were formerly in the collection of the Earl of Strathmore at Gibside, Co Durham, and have the name Gibside stamped on the underside of the seat rails. The beechwood chairs are decorated with black and gold japanning, notably of a type that has no chinoiserie motifs but is formed of scrolling gilt acanthus leaves and classical garlands on a black background. There appears to be an 'S' motif, for Strathmore, at the centre of

262 Designed for use as a wine cooler, this mahogany container is lined with lead and placed on a stand.

263 (opposite) These Regency library chairs are soberly derived in design from classical models, but are also equipped with delightful book rests and candle sconces.

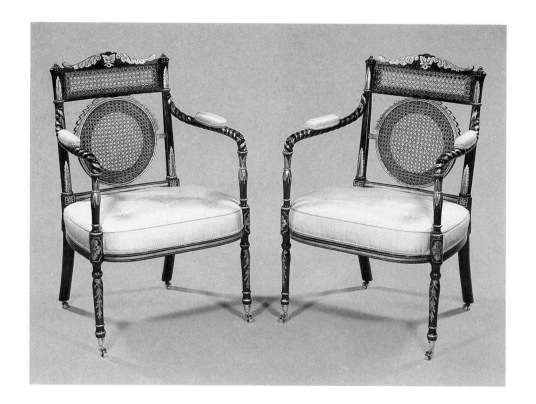

the back rail of each chair. A fine bookcase of circa 1810 (fig 264) is made of coromandel or calamander wood, which has strong markings, even more so than rosewood. The natural figuration and colour of the wood is contrasted by neat brass mouldings around the drawer fronts and glass panes of the bookcase. In the lower part of the cabinet, the doors are faced with brass trellis grills, another popular feature of Regency furniture. This was sometimes left open and more often lined with silk. The bookcase stands on small cast brass paw feet.

Another piece showing an interesting use of wood is a sofa table of burr oak made in about 1830 (fig 266). Here the light, densely figured veneers are contrasted with a simple inlay of ebony lines and with carved ebony mouldings around the drawer fronts and rosettes on the scroll supports of the central platform pedestal. Reeded legs terminate in gilt brass acanthus toes and castors. A handsome writing table of about the same date (fig 267), stands on four sturdy reeded tapering legs, crowned at the top with classical lions' heads with rings in their mouths as if to have a rope attached. A bold, flowing key pattern design is indented around the sides of the table. A bookcase of very interesting form is shown in fig 268. This shallow cabinet

264 (opposite) An early 19th-century bookcase of coromandel or calamander wood, the strong markings of which are cleanly outlined with neat brass mouldings.

265 These chairs, made for the Earl of Strathmore, are based on a design by Thomas Sheraton. They are of beech decorated in black and gold.

266 A sofa-table of burr oak, decorated solely with ebony lines and rosettes on the base, circa 1830.

267 A Greek key pattern around the frieze of this Regency writing table gives a fashionable look to this otherwise traditional Georgian design.

268 Elegant tiered shelving, supported by brass columns, form a superstructure to a long mahogany cabinet, circa 1810.

269 Brass lines, mouldings, feet and knobs add smartness to the contrasting rosewood and kingwood of a Regency drum table of semi-classical form, akin to French Empire furniture.

consists of tiered shelves in decreasing size above a line of cupboards with contrasting shaped door fronts. Brasswork in the base and especially brass columns supporting the shelves give a lightness of design and at the top of the cabinet there is a pierced brass gallery with finials on it.

A rosewood drum table (fig 269) stands on an interesting tripod base with a central vase shaped stem supported by three scrolling buttresses. It combines contrasting woods with brass line inlay which was another popular feature of Regency furniture. The brass line in the top is punctuated with star shaped forms and drawer fronts are inset with linear patterns. The handles of the drawers are also in the form of Regency stars. The feet of the table are colossal brass claws.

270 A Regency convex mirror, flanked by glass candle sconces, is apparently suspended by ribbons and a family crest. It is one of a pair of about 1810.

Amongst fine giltwood furniture of the Regency period may be noted a pair of circular convex mirrors in giltwood frames with mahogany fillets around the glass (fig 270). Circular mirrors of this type were another popular feature of early 19th-century interiors but this is an especially remarkable pair. Carved giltwood ribbons, effortlessly tied in a bow at the top, decorate heraldic crests, ostriches with horse-shoes in their beaks, representing the patron for whom they were made – in this case apparently Lord Digby, though the mirrors are reputed to have come from Stoke Edith, Herefordshire, home of the Foley family. From these birds are also suspended, unusually, swags of cut glass drops, while on either side of the mirrors there are candle arms holding cut glass sconces with hanging drops.

271 Reflecting both classical origins and campaign furniture, 'X' frame chairs and stools became a feature of smart early 19th-century houses. This one is made up of wondrous serpent-like birds.

Returning to ideas derived from Greece and Rome is the X frame chair. This kind of construction had already been popular in medieval England and was consistently used as a practical form until the age of oak. Now, however, with more direct reference to the ancients, the shape was taken up again as an archetypal element in 19th-century neo-classicism. The chair in fig 271 has an X frame consisting of winged birds and, strangely, hairy legs with paws. Entirely executed in carved giltwood, it is a most unusual piece.

Chinoiserie played a major part in early 19th-century decoration; the Royal Pavilion at Brighton, built for the Prince Regent, is a most exotic and whimsical *tour de force* of opulent frivolity. 'Indian' domes enclose rooms of Georgian proportion encrusted with fanciful oriental decoration; the sheer

272 Tôle panels (tin), decorated with extravagant chinoiseries in several shades of gilding, were used for the doors of this delightful Regency cabinet. Borders of red japanning frame the doors.

fun of the place is encapsulated within its endless attempt to represent oriental mysteries in semi-humorous guise. Too much furniture is loosely and wrongly said to be derived from the Royal Pavilion, but there is certainly a notable body of fine Regency furniture of a style and quality comparable to works of art there.

Unidentified, as yet, is a maker of furniture who incorporated tole panels richly decorated with chinoiseries in tones of gold on red and black. A cabinet from this school (fig 272) contains tôle panels in the doors, and a tôle top and sides within a wooden framework. Inside is a series of drawers with magnificent red an gold decoration also worked on metal plates. The quality of the painting here, and on the outside of the cabinet, is extremely good, japanning at its best. It combines direct imitations of Chinese lacquer together with an English combination of flowers and patterns woven together in the borders. Also of tôle is a charming pair of small face screens (fig 273). These are decorated with multicoloured chinoiseries on a black ground. The screens can be moved up and down according to the height of a candle for which there is a sconce behind. A little drawer in each plinth allows for the storage of matches.

273 A pair of tôle screens for table use, to shield faces from excessive heat from a fire. Candles on the other side would illumine a book.

The chaise longue in fig 274 is one of a pair and part of a suite of furniture drawn in the neo-classical manner with slightly outward splaying sabre-shaped legs at one end. The beechwood frame is japanned in black and gold with a panel of chinoiserie in an oval at the footrest. Another good pair of armchairs, again part of a set (fig 275), is eminently typical of the Regency period. Of beechwood, they are decorated in black with water-gilt enrichments and have ovals in the backs, this time not filled with chinoiserie but with grisaille vignettes in a classical mode. In a vaguely Graeco-Roman manner the arms are supported by animal legs while the trellis in the backs is more a feature of the Far East. The overall proportion and design is most charming and successful despite the decorative elements being derived from such an extraordinary mixture. The chair reflects the influence of the campaigns and military exploits of Napoleon and others.

A folding bed of brass and steel (fig 276) undoubtedly derives from such travelling. It is capable of being packed into a case for easy transport. The carpet around the bed is also French of about 1810.

274 and 275 (opposite) Regency furniture designs were inspired by surveys of classical and Egyptian artefacts witnessed on military campaigns. This seat furniture, decorated in black and gold, has elements of each, while the bed above (fig 276) is of steel and brass, for use on campaign.

Very different, and very English in their severe Grecian classicism, is a pair of large scale blue-john urns (fig 278). Blue-john, or Derbyshire fluorspar, was only mined in England and these urns are unusually large and fine examples of many pieces that were made of the material. Here the chosen form is a boldly stylised Grecian vase. The insides have been hollowed out and one supposes that a candle may well have been lit inside in order to shine through and show off the semi-transparent stone. The vases are set on black marble plinths.

A pair of large tub chairs in the manner of a less well known cabinet-maker, George Smith (fig 279), has a relatively plain line but the chairs are supported at the front by grand, monopoid lions whose gilded masks form the armrests. A classical laurel wreath moulding follows the seat frame at the base. Of exceptional Georgian elegance is the hexagonal hall lantern in fig 277. One of a pair, it is in patinated brass with finely cast gilt metal decoration and with classical palmettes and scrolled acanthus leaves about cluster columns. Glass smoke cowls are suspended above the lanterns.

277 (opposite) While still of Georgian proportions, this lantern is ornamented with gothic clustre columns and a wealth of classical decoration. One of a pair, circa 1810.

278 A pair of Grecian-shaped urns of Derbyshire fluorspar or blue-john, circa 1825.

279 These large tub chairs are supported by bold monopoid Egyptian lions.

Revivals of medieval gothic decoration occurred from time to time in the 17th and 18th centuries but none was so great as that of the early 19th century in England. Pugin was the high priest of this style and his work on the rebuilt Houses of Parliament in collaboration with Charles Barry is justly celebrated. As always, styles of architecture influenced and led styles of furniture. The charming side-cabinet circa 1840 in fig 280 shows many elements of gothic decoration in its fine carving as well as its overall form. The sinuous pierced carving in the back is reminiscent of the 16th-century oak furniture which itself developed from medieval gothic architecture. The carving around the table base of the cabinet seems to be derived from Renaissance ideas, thereby contributing to a typically Victorian eclectic synthesis.

A handsome brass lantern (fig 282) of hexagonal form and Georgian proportions is conceived in high gothic style. Floreate arches cap each glazed side and are filled with interesting tracery.

Another interesting early 19th-century form of decoration was penwork — decoration which appeared to resemble engraved ivory or filigree ivory inlay. White painting was done on a black background or vice versa and was often,

280 (opposite, above) The gothic extravagance of this cabinet is derived from both medieval architecture and early oak furniture (circa 1840)

281 (opposite, below) The amateur decoration of these cabinets of 1842-5 is of black and white 'pen-work', and with colourful scenes and posies on the interiors.

282 (above) A brass lantern with high-gothic tracery.

I believe, executed by amateurs. A delightful pair of cabinets in this technique is shown in fig 281. The two pieces consist of cupboards containing a variety of drawers, different in each case, on stands with cabriole legs. The external decoration is of complex black and white floral patterns with trellis-work on the sides. The interiors of the doors and the drawer fronts are beautifully painted in polychromes. In one case the decoration is of colourful flower sprigs and posies, while the other shows a fascinating post-card-type collection of scenes including King's College, Cambridge and a number of holiday resorts in the North of England. This work is inscribed: 'Commenced Painting this Cabinet September 24th 1842. Finished May 23rd 1845. Augusta M. Alderson'. Augusta Alderson was the daughter of a rector in Yorkshire; the rectory and Harthill Church are depicted twice.

The delightful pair of tilt-top occasional tables circa 1840 in fig 283 is japanned in black and gold; the turned bases and scrolling legs being finely decorated with gilt chinoiseries. The rectangular tops, however, contain still life paintings of fruits, charmingly executed and framed within a chinoiserie border. This may also be amateur work.

A colossal mid 19th-century globe must have been made for a library (fig 284). A Regency style mahogany base with brass mouldings contains the

283 A pair of black japanned occasional tables, with still life paintings on the tilting tops.

284 A large library globe, supported by a mahogany and brass stand,
circa 1840.

splendid four-foot diameter terrestrial sphere. Of a similar date, perhaps around 1860, is a fine quality kidney-shape desk, veneered in walnut, with marquetry reminiscent of late 17th-century Holland (fig 285), thereby bringing us back in full circle to the Dutch marquetry of the William and Mary period described at the beginning of this book. Even at the back of the knee-hole section there is a panel containing a vase of flowers in marquetry. The desk is further enriched with gilt brass mounts and a pierced brass gallery around the back of the writing surface which is lined with leather.

Rather different in feeling, but also of about 1850, is a pair of Jacobean-style side-chairs (fig 286). These chairs, following late 17th-century antecedents, are of oak with turned barley-sugar legs and backs. The tops of the backs contain a carved coat of arms within scrollwork and grapes. The needlework panels on the backs of the chair are original while the seats are of the period, but replacements. The spirit of this furniture successfully demonstrates a revival that was, at least in part, an attempt to create an atmosphere of antiquarianism with over-riding nuances of historical permanence. Part of the glory of great antique furniture has always been its allusion to the past linked with true worthiness and lasting appeal dependent on style and quality.

285 A Victorian kidney-shaped kneehole desk inlaid with marquetry, a revival of the Dutch marquetry adopted by England at the end of the 17th century.

286 Antiquarianism, rather than revival, inspired this Victorian re-phrasing of a Jacobean style. Of oak, the chairs are well carved with heraldic arms and with traditional 'barley-sugar' turned supports (circa 1880).

247

```
┌─────────────────────────────────────┐
│  ┌───────────────────────────────┐  │
│  │                               │  │
│  │        COLLECTIONS            │  │
│  │                               │  │
│  └───────────────────────────────┘  │
└─────────────────────────────────────┘
```

*M*ost of the magnificent pieces of furniture described and illustrated here were purchased from Mallett's by private clients for their own collections, and so are not readily available for viewing. It is hoped, however, that the owners will be pleased to allow readers of this book to share this documentation of them.

I have mentioned that Mallett's has also supplied works of art to many museums, and items that were once in our galleries may now be seen in a good many countries. The important commode by Jean-Henri Riesener, shown in fig 146, is on view at the Art Institute of Chicago, and a considerable number of other pieces of furniture and objects are now to be seen in public collections.

The most significant corpus of English furniture is of course the magnificent collection at the Victoria and Albert Museum, London. Among the wonders there are some 55 pieces which have come from Mallett's over the years. These include both large and smaller items. Other pieces are now in the remarkable collection of English furniture and decorative arts at the Metropolitan Museum of Art in New York. Included in that museum is Judge Irwin Untermyer's collection, which includes several items from Mallett's. The museum at Colonial Williamsburg includes very fine embroideries which are recorded in our photographic archives, and many other articles have found their way to city and provincial museums in England and the United

287 Emblematic of the restrained glories of English furniture is this Queen Anne walnut bureau bookcase, of perfect proportions, of the finest wood and of a superb colour. It is fitted with many compartments and secret drawers (circa 1710).

States of America. Other pieces have gone to continental museums including the Rijksmuseum, Amsterdam, and at least one item to a museum in Japan.

Sometimes collectors who bought from us have later generously given furniture to public institutions. The Terry Collection in York is remarkable for carved mahogany furniture some of which was acquired from Mallett's. Dr Goodhart's remarkable collection of 17th and 18th century needlework samplers was formed in conjunction with Mallett's and is now to be seen at Montacute House, Somerset, a property of the National Trust. Another National Trust property is Basildon Park, Berkshire. Amongst magnificent furniture there, acquired through this business, is a most remarkable pair of giltwood side tables with marquetry tops together with pier glasses en suite. These tables travelled all the way to Washington for the great Treasure Houses of Britain Exhibition at the National Gallery of Art in 1985. Also now belonging to the National Trust is the superb suite of needlework furniture made from Canons Ashby, Northamptonshire, and partly illustrated in fig 218. A notable textile item handled by Mallett's and later acquired by the nation independently, and now to be seen again at the National Trust's Oxburgh Hall, Norfolk, is the assembly of 16th-century needlework panels known as the Oxburgh hangings. These were worked by Mary Queen of Scots, Bess of Hardwick and others during the Earl of Shrewsbury's custodianship of Mary Queen of Scots. Francis Egerton took the hangings up to Scotland to be scrutinised by Sir William Burrell through a huge magnifying glass, but he rejected them.

Other furniture from Mallett's may be seen at the Bowes Museum, Castle Barnard, Co. Durham; Temple Newsam, Leeds; Mompesson House, Salisbury; and Bristol Museum and Art Gallery.

When describing the splendid clock by Matthew Boulton (fig 242) I mentioned that it has now found a permanent home in the Courtauld Gallery at Somerset House, London. Also recently acquired by this institution and incorporated into its new location at Somerset House is an important architectural furniture fitment, a medal cabinet designed by Sir William Chambers for the Earl of Charlemont for Charlemont House, Dublin in 1767. It is made of mahogany, sandalwood and boxwood, possibly by Chippendale as his name is inscribed alongside the design. It was pleasing to reflect upon the original craftsmen when it was the turn of our own Mallett cabinet-makers to instal this impressive piece, most appropriately, in Chambers' magnificent Somerset House.

*288 An Adam girondole, a giltwood wall appliqué supporting two
candles, circa 1780.*

INDEX